New Science
New Brain
New You

Also by Eve Delunas

Survival Games Personalities Play

New Science
New Brain
New You

Eve Delunas, PhD

With love and gratitude to my dear friend
Dr. Sue A. Cooper, who provided the seed of inspiration
for this book and nurtured it to fruition.

Contents

CONTENTS

Exercises

Acknowledgements

I am grateful to Ute Bender and Dr. Sue A. Cooper for their review of the manuscript and many helpful suggestions for improvement. I am blessed to have such wise and gifted healers as friends!

I also wish to acknowledge my sisters, Cynthia Miller and Andrea Mosca, who have taught me much about love by their example and who are such a source of support for me.

A big "thank you" goes to Elisabeth Rinaldi, whose editorial prowess made this a much better book. I also extend my deepest appreciation to Beth Skelley for creating the beautiful cover and book design. It was pleasure to work with two such talented professionals who put both heart and soul into their work.

I am fortunate to share my life with an amazing man who also happens to be a terrific writer. My husband, Dr. Roger Stilgenbauer, was the first to read and offer feedback on this manuscript and he also provided the title for this book. Thank you, Roger, for the love and laughter you bring into my life every day.

Lastly, I wish to thank all of the special people I have seen in my psychotherapy practice who have taught me so much about the beauty and resilience of the human spirit.

Introduction

Willpower is grossly overrated as a means to change. Oh, sure, it works fine for the little things. We can will ourselves to remember to floss our teeth, take our vitamins, or eat more vegetables. But to change habitual, maladaptive ways of thinking, feeling, or behaving, relying on willpower alone doesn't work for most of us—just look at how many of us follow through with our New Year's resolutions for longer than a few weeks. When it comes to relinquishing long-standing habits or troublesome addictions, our efforts to force ourselves to change only fuel an internal battle that makes us feel increasingly out of control. Too often, we end up doing *more* of the very thing we are trying to *stop* doing. Even as we vow to refrain from eating so much sugar, we find ourselves downing a second or third candy bar.

Why is this? Because using willpower works *against* our own biology. Thanks to new research tools which track the brain's activities, such as PET scans, functional MRI scans (fMRI), and SPECT scans, we now know our brains have a kind of "default-functioning mode" that is based upon our life experiences—particularly those from our early years. This default mode is programmed into the part of the brain that is associated with emotion, memory, and motivation. When we try to change ingrained, negative behaviors by using willpower alone, it's like trying to alter the automatic functions on a computer without changing the default settings. To create lasting changes in how we think, feel, and behave, we must reconfigure our brain's default setting which is encoded in the parts of the brain that are not entirely within our conscious awareness.

In my thirty-year career as a psychotherapist, I have found that talk therapy alone is usually insufficient for readjusting our brains' default settings. This is because our dysfunctional selves easily coexist with the rational, practical, thinking parts of us—though each operates on a different agenda. For example, while our logical self may recognize that our out-of-control spending is sabotaging our happiness by drowning us in credit card debt, at a deeper level we feel compelled to continue the very behavior that is creating our suffering.

When talk therapy alone does not alleviate long-standing, self-defeating habits, I have found that a method called *guided imagery* works remarkably well to catalyze desired changes. Recently, neuropsychology has provided explanations as to how and why guided imagery is so effective. The holistic language of guided imagery—that of symbols, pictures, sounds, smells, tastes, physical sensations, stories, patterns, and analogies—is the same "language" that is recognized by the parts of the brain that have encoded the thoughts, feelings, and images associated with our default modes of functioning.

This *new brain science* has provided evidence of our brain's ability to grow new neurons and engage new brain pathways, even in our adult years. Using guided imagery, we can stimulate the formation of alternate brain connections that enable us to change easily, rather than through the excessive use of will or force. These new brain pathways liberate us to respond in creative and life-affirming ways to the same old situations.

Alternate ways of thinking, feeling, and behaving begin to feel more natural and automatic than the old behaviors we are replacing. Instead of coming home from work and sinking into the couch in front of the television, Mona is inspired to change clothes and go for a brisk walk on a lovely evening. Rather than procrastinating on a difficult project at work for fear of not doing a good enough job, Vince feels motivated to begin working on it early by asking for help from other team members and acting on their recommendations. When her seventh-grade son brings home a progress report that indicates he's failing science,

Nina easily avoids blowing her top—her old reaction pattern. Instead, she initiates a conversation later in the day, when she is feeling calm, open to listening to him, and eager to explore viable solutions.

When we use guided imagery to reset our default mode, we work *with* rather than *against* our own biology: the inspiration and motivation to change our behavior emerges from within us and feels natural—in sync with who we are and what we want for ourselves. There is no inner battleground, no sense of the need to force ourselves to do what we do not want to do. Since change happens more easily and organically, we feel that all our parts are in alignment with one another. We are at one with ourselves and feel that our transformation is powered from within.

I have written this book to share with you the guided imagery methods that work particularly well for removing old limitations and inviting new possibilities into your life. The capacity to change lies within you and awaits your activation. By exploring your vast, inner landscape, you can unleash your potential, find your own answers, and tap into a wellspring of courage, inspiration, and motivation that can propel you in new directions.

I hope this book will also be a resource for counselors, psychologists, marriage therapists, hypnotherapists, and coaches, to use with their clients. I know, like me, many professionals recognize both the value and the limitations of traditional talk therapy and are seeking other alternatives. Although readers can use these guided imagery processes on their own, there is a special benefit that comes from doing this work with a trained professional who can offer support and guidance to the one who has chosen to embark on this journey of healing and self-realization.

A new you lies within, waiting for you to discover it! I wish you much joy and fulfillment as you invite this more evolved and "updated" version of yourself to take center stage in your life.

The Spellbound Brain

Melinda is an attractive professional woman in her early fifties who came to me for therapy after she and her third husband had decided to divorce. As she spoke of her failed marriages with much anger, frustration, hurt, and sadness, I noticed that she said, "He turned his back on me" in describing what went wrong in each relationship. I asked Melinda to close her eyes, relax, and tell me about the first time someone she loved turned his or her back on her. Within moments, Melinda tearfully described being abandoned as a three-year-old on her father's doorstep as her mother turned and walked away, not to re-enter her life for several years. Further exploration revealed that Melinda's father and a number of other adults whom she loved and trusted had also repeatedly turned their backs on her during her childhood.

As an adult, Melinda has unconsciously re-created the theme of her childhood in each of her marriages. It is not that Melinda has intentionally set out to have her husbands disappoint, reject, and turn their backs on her both emotionally and physically. Indeed, Melinda wants desperately to have a successful, loving, mutually supportive relationship with a man. However, when it comes to intimate relationships, Melinda operates in accordance with thoughts, feelings, and beliefs about herself and those she loves which were first encoded in her brain during her early years. Terrified that her partner will leave her,

Melinda becomes smothering, unduly suspicious, and overly controlling. Eventually, this behavior drives each partner to do what she fears most: turn his back on her. Melinda's default mode regarding intimate relationships has not yet been reset to accommodate the newer and wiser perspective of her current, adult self.

The Spellbound State

Like Melinda, many of us are impacted by our brains' maladaptive default settings that keep us from living more joyful and fulfilling lives. I call this being *spellbound*. A sign that we are spellbound is that, in spite of our desire to change and our best efforts to do so, we repeatedly engage in the same self-defeating behaviors that lead to the same distressing results. Bryant continues to fall in love with women who are not interested in him. Sonya works harder than anyone else in her office, but fails to advocate for herself and continues to be passed over for promotion year after year. Jordan keeps returning to drinking, though he vows to quit each time his wife threatens to leave him and take the children. Derrick has put up with a string of bosses who treat him in a demeaning and disrespectful fashion. Reyna is always in debt and has already declared bankruptcy twice. Nick has violent outbursts that have gotten him fired and that have led to his arrest on several occasions. Marina has almost lost her children twice due to reports of child abuse. Sherrill is morbidly obese but cannot seem to stop overeating, despite her doctor's warnings that she is on a fast track to a heart attack or stroke.

Most of us who are spellbound are not aware that we are being negatively impacted by our personal history. Typically, we believe we have put the past behind us and moved on, and that prior life experiences have no impact on our lives in the present. Why aren't we aware that the past has its hold on us when we are spellbound? What causes our spellbound state and what can we do to overcome it? The answers to these questions lie in discoveries in the exciting, new field of neuropsychology, often called *the new brain science*.

Experience Sculpts the Brain

One of the most important findings in the past few decades is the fact that our brains are sculpted by our life experiences.[1] As humans, our brains share certain key components, although each one of our brains is completely unique because it is the sum total of all we have lived. There are endless variations in the ways our brains develop and, consequently, in how they operate since the functioning of our brains is determined by their structure. What's more, since our minds work in accordance with our brains, the structure of our brains has much to do with our typical ways of thinking, feeling, and acting.

All this points to the vital role experience plays in our brains' development. It is our experience—our interaction with our social, physical, and cultural environment—that stimulates our brains to create new connections between nerve cells, which are called *neurons*. These connections, or synapses, form the pathways by which parts of our brains communicate with their other parts. Ultimately, our brains form trillions of synapses, as each of the eighty to one hundred billion neurons located therein establishes connections to ten thousand or more other neurons.

Our unique experiences are recorded in our memory banks, and as this happens, our brains are sculpted through the formation and strengthening of new neural networks. Neuropsychologists have determined that our brains record two kinds of memories. Beginning at birth or even before birth, our brains encode *implicit*, or nondeclarative, memories with the help of the part of the brain called the *amygdala*.[2] Around the age of one and a half to two years old, our brains begin encoding *explicit*, or declarative, memories, while also continuing to record implicit memories.[3]

Implicit memories are nonverbal recollections that are encoded in the brain without our conscious recognition that we are inputting data into our memory banks. Our implicit memories consist of feeling states, perceptions, bodily sensations, and behavioral responses. Beginning in infancy, implicit memories of being touched, held, bathed, fed, or spoken to are recorded in our brains in the form of new brain connections. As we grow, our brains take note of the kinds of interactions we have with those familiar and unfamiliar to us, our physical activities, our bodily states, and the world as we perceive it through our five senses. Implicit memories are intriguing because we don't know when we are storing them, and we also are not aware when an implicit memory has been activated in our brains. Although we are recalling something from our past, we have no conscious awareness that we are doing so.[4]

Explicit memories begin to form once the part of the brain called the *hippocampus* starts to develop along with the prefrontal cortex. These memories are verbal and often involve the autobiographical details of our lives. For example, you may recall a childhood trip to Disneyland, your first day attending a new school, or your mother bringing home a new baby brother or sister from the hospital. Explicit memories require our attention in order for them to be encoded in our brains; and when we bring explicit memories to mind, we have the conscious recognition that we are doing so. In processing explicit memories, the hippocampus and the prefrontal cortex help us gain a greater perspective by making associations that place the event in a larger context. The hippocampus integrates the various segments of the memory—the perceptions, sensations, somatic (physical) experiences, emotions, and thoughts—into a meaningful narrative by engaging many other brain structures in this encoding process, including the prefrontal cortex, which specializes in higher level thought.[5] For example, in recalling a visit to your grandparents' house, you may consciously remember the feel of your grandmother's arms wrapped around you as she greets you, the smell of her cooking, the sound of your grandfather's voice, or the sense of safety and comfort that you derived from being there.

Mental Models Are Derived from Implicit Memories

An important aspect of implicit memories is that they form the basis of our *mental models*—the mindsets we use to make sense of our world.[6] Our mental models, also called *schemas*, are generalizations about ourselves, about others, about relationships, and about the world we live in, which are based upon our life experiences—particularly those from our early years. For example, if we were well cared for in infancy and early childhood, we probably operate from a mental model that other people are worthy of trust. If we were abandoned, neglected, or abused in infancy and early childhood, our schemas probably include the perspective that other people cannot be trusted.

For the most part, these mental models remain outside of our conscious awareness, although they play a significant role in determining our unique reality. In fact, these mental models are so much a part of us that we don't even recognize them for what they are. Instead, we hold them as the "truth" about ourselves, others, and the world, not realizing the degree to which they impact our expectations, color our perceptions, dampen or intensify our enthusiasm for life, and guide our choices.

As we go through our childhood years, our interactions—both positive and negative—with parents, siblings, peers, and others impact our mental models. Serena was teased relentlessly by her classmates for her size, the color of her skin, and her thick accent, and concluded that she was ugly and unlovable. Manfred was the best in his school in sports, and concluded that he is a strong and capable athlete. Roland, who suffered from undiagnosed dyslexia that made learning to read very difficult for him, concluded that he was stupid. Damien, who was treated like a prince by his single mother, came to expect that his needs were more important than anyone else's.

Trauma Leads to Maladaptive Schemas

We are likely to develop maladaptive mental models when we experience events that are traumatic for us; for example, the death or departure of a loved one; becoming ill; surviving an automobile accident; experiencing a natural disaster such as an earthquake, hurricane, flood, or fire; being physically beaten or raped; witnessing or hearing about any form of violence or destruction; being emotionally, physically, or sexually abused; being neglected or abandoned caregivers;

being the victim of prejudice or discrimination; or, being repeatedly teased, humiliated, or rejected by caregivers, siblings, or peers.

Because of differences in life experiences and personality characteristics, each of us may be negatively impacted by certain events that may not be remarkable or upsetting to someone else. Trauma is individually defined, and therefore, personal. It is important to note that two individuals can have the same or similar early life experiences and develop very different mental models as a result of those events. It is not the event itself that determines our mental models; it is the child's unique interpretation of those events. For example, in a family in which the parents have frequent violent arguments, one child may unconsciously conclude that it is her job to keep peace in the family at all costs, while another decides to always be strong and capable so she can defend herself against aggressors. Still another child in the same family may come to believe that her parents' fights are her fault and that it is because she is bad or "not good enough."

It is more likely that we will be traumatized by the events of our childhood and adolescence than by those of our adulthood. We are more vulnerable to the negative impact of distressful events in our childhood because, as children, we have fewer resources for dealing with painful circumstances. The fewer resources we have to cope with a painful event, the more likely it is to be traumatic for us. Thus, it usually takes more extreme circumstances to traumatize an adult than it does a child.

Schemas Govern our Default-Functioning Mode

Each of us has numerous mental models. The schemas that are positive serve us very well, as they enable us to make life-affirming choices and guide us toward healthy relationships and joyful lives. If you consider yourself to be a capable person who deserves respect, that is what you will choose for yourself. If you find yourself in a situation that is otherwise, you are likely to sense that it is not right for you and either do something to change the situation or find the exit door. Similarly, if you believe that most people are fundamentally good and worthy of trust, you will probably allow certain others to get close to you. This does not mean you will trust everyone—nor does it mean that you will always make good choices for yourself. But overall, your default-functioning mode is one of *openness* and *expansion*. You choose to open to new life experiences that afford you the opportunity to grow, to express your uniqueness, and to feel fully engaged in life. When you do make a wrong turn, you eventually discover that you're off course, and will use your own inner navigational tools to find your way back to the life path that leads you where you want to go.

When we have negative, limiting mental models, we operate with false data that misleads us by distorting our perceptions, lowering our expectations, and misguiding our choices. Unconsciously, we delete information that is counter to our mental models and form generalizations that do not account for life's infinite variations. Our schemas serve as reality filters that automatically screen out any information that is counter to our worldview. If our mental model is one that brands us as unlovable, then we will completely miss or misinterpret the countless ways those dear to us may attempt to convey their affection. If we hold the schema that life is nothing but a painful struggle, then we will fail to register any opportunities that come our way to let it be easier, and we will continue to make choices that validate that worldview. We think our mental models are accurate because we always make ourselves "right" by seeing what we expect to see, experiencing what we expect to experience, and making choices which are in alignment with our distorted view of ourselves, others, and life in general.

Maladaptive Schemas Cause Us to Be Spellbound

When we have maladaptive mental models, our default mode is one of *blockage* and *constriction*. Rather than opening to new life experiences, we cling to the familiar. Spellbound, we are driven by fear and, in our efforts to protect ourselves from pain, engage repeatedly in the same self-defeating behaviors. We choose the path that we hope will ensure our safety, rather than the one with the greatest promise of joy and fulfillment. The result is the opposite of what we are trying to achieve—we end up suffering more not less. James believes others he loves will always leave him; the walls he has put around his heart to prevent others from hurting him have caused him to live a lonely and empty life. Zeke doubts his capacity to make wise choices. His refusal to commit himself to a course of action may keep him from failing, but it also has caused him to stagnate in his life. Krystal believes she is not good enough to pursue her dream of having a career as a graphic artist. She continues to take jobs she hates and manages to keep herself too busy to pursue her life's passion.

One former client of mine held the mental model "I am worthless" due to a painful childhood fraught with loss, neglect, and maltreatment. Believing she was devoid of value, she became a hard-core drug addict, prostituted herself for drugs, had one abusive relationship after another, and managed to destroy anything good that ever happened to her. At a deep level, beyond words, she felt that she did not deserve any better—and we typically get what we believe we deserve. Eventually, this client recognized what was happening, sought therapy, and managed to completely turn her life around.

Change Is Always Possible

If you recognize yourself in these descriptions, it is important, first and foremost, not to judge or berate yourself. You have been doing the best you could with what you know. There is no reason to feel guilty or ashamed for having made choices you later regret. That is part of the human condition. Each path you have followed has made you the person you are today, and each experience you have lived has in some way deepened, enriched, strengthened, or opened you to your greater potential. Life is not a contest and there is nowhere that we are "supposed" to be except exactly where we are in this moment. Remind yourself that your power to change lies in the present—and allow yourself to look ahead rather than behind. No matter what you have lived, you have the ability to point your life in a brand new direction beginning today. There are simple strategies you can use to reset your default mode. This book will show you how to do that step-by-step, with practical tools to rewire your brain and catalyze the emergence of a new you.

The Brain Can Rewire Itself at Any Age

Recent advancements in neuroscience confirm that the brain is capable of learning new patterns and forming alternate neuronal pathways well into old age. We call this ability for the brain to rewire itself and generate new neural connections *experience-dependent-neuroplasticity*.[7] Several Nobel Prize winners have contributed to our knowledge of the brain's ability to change itself. First, Donald Hebb, a Canadian neuropsychologist, is credited with the discovery that "neurons that fire together, wire together."[8] In 2000, the American neuroscientist Eric Kandel won the Nobel Prize in Physiology or Medicine for his research on the ways in which the brain creates new synapses when learning takes place. Our brains develop in accordance to what we are experiencing. As we repeatedly entertain certain thoughts, feelings, and sensations, our brain grows new neuronal connections.[9] This means that we can use our minds to change our brains; our thoughts actually change the ways in which the neurons in our brains communicate with one another and are able to stimulate the creation of new brain connections—regardless of our age.

Research over the past few years has also called into question the long-held notion that adults are incapable of generating new brain cells. An increasing body of evidence shows that the adult brain can engage in *neurogenesis*—the ability to grow new neurons from neuronal stem cells. In one German study, a group of twenty-four adults were recruited. Half of them were taught to juggle, and instructed to practice the new skill daily for three months, while the other half did no juggling. In sophisticated pre- and post-tests conducted to measure grey matter in the parts of the brain associated with visual and motor activity, it was found that the jugglers had an increase in both brain volume and density in these regions. Incidentally, once they stopped juggling, participants' brains returned to their original sizes within three months.[10] Another study documented the increase in grey matter among twenty research subjects who learned Buddhist insight meditation and practiced it forty minutes a day.[11]

Each of us has the ability to grow new brain cells and establish new brain networks that enable us to think, feel, and behave differently—no matter how long we have felt stuck, no matter how many times we have tried to change and failed, no matter how hopeless and helpless we feel. Let's look more closely at how you can create long-lasting changes in your brain that will open up a world of new possibilities for you.

While the information presented in the following sections is technical, it provides the key for understanding when and how we become spellbound, and what we can do about it. By taking a closer look at the parts of the brain and how they operate, you can identify both the origins of your automatic behaviors and the most effective ways to change your default-functioning mode.

The Triune Brain

Thanks to the work of Paul MacLean, MD, the brain is generally seen as functioning in three separate, interconnected parts, each with its own area of specialization and form of intelligence.[12] These include the oldest part of the brain at the base of the spine, often called the *reptilian brain* or *old brain*; the *midbrain*, which sits just above that and is often called the *limbic system*; and the new brain, which consists of the grey matter called the *neocortex* or *cerebral cortex* that covers the other structures. The reptilian brain controls and supports essential functions vital for sustaining life such as breathing and the heartbeat. It is also involved to some extent with wakefulness, sleep, balance, coordination, and simple actions that require little thought once they have been learned.[13]

The limbic system, the second part of the human brain to evolve, deals with sensations, motivation, and emotions. It regulates hormonal states, blood pressure, blood sugar levels, digestion, and body temperature as it monitors our interactions with the social environment. The midbrain, along with the reptilian brain, controls the autonomic nervous system that is responsible for our fight, flight, faint, or freeze reaction in times of perceived danger. The hippocampus (mentioned earlier) is a part of the limbic system and helps to process autobiographical and factual memories by creating cognitive maps that place memories in context with their associated emotions, sensations, perceptions, and an accompanying verbal narrative.[14] The amygdala, predominantly involved in the encoding of implicit memories, is also a part of the midbrain. The amygdala is where emotional memories appear to be stored and emotional states like anger, aggression, fear, and sadness are regulated. The amygdala is important for our survival and serves as the body's warning system in times of danger by activating a physical response even before we are conscious that there is a potential problem. For example, perhaps you have had the experience of slamming the brakes on your car before your mind registers that the car ahead has come to an abrupt stop.[15]

The grey matter that covers our brain, our neocortex or cerebral cortex, was the last part of the brain to develop. It enables us to perform the higher mental functions associated with being human, like applying logic to solve a problem, composing a beautiful piece of music, planning a vacation, analyzing our tax returns, or communicating with others through writing or speech. With its help, we are able to conceptualize, reflect, and derive meaning from our experiences. The forefront of the frontal lobe, called the prefrontal cortex, is the part of the cerebral cortex that is considered the most advanced or evolved. While the cerebral cortex's influence on our thoughts, feelings, and behavior is significant, we must not underestimate the vital role played by the activity of the limbic system and brain stem in providing information about our social environment, our somatic states, and our emotional reactions, to the cortex.

One part of the brain that develops very early in life and appears to play an essential role in mediating signals between the old brain, limbic system, and cortex is located behind our eyes and is called the orbitofrontal cortex (OFC). The OFC is considered a part of both the limbic system and the prefrontal cortex. The OFC has garnered a great deal of attention recently because it is ideally situated to connect with all three regions of the brain at the same time. Dr. Daniel Siegel, a psychiatrist and neurobiology researcher, and Mary Hartzell, an early-childhood educator, write, "The orbitofrontal cortex is the only area of the brain that is one synapse away from all three major regions of the brain."[16] This means it is like a central processing unit, sending and receiving neural impulses from the cortex, the limbic system, and the brain stem to coordinate their efforts. "The orbitofrontal cortex is the ultimate neural integrating convergence zone of the brain"[17]

In particular, research indicates that the OFC has a close connection with the amygdala, which is the part of the brain known to regulate strong emotions like anger and fear. The OFC is also closely aligned with the parts of the limbic system that enable us to be emotionally attuned to others in interpersonal relationships. The OFC develops in the context of safe, supportive, and trusting early relationships and, with its development, a person benefits from a greater ability to regulate his or her emotions and to relate to others in social situations.[18] Siegel and Harzell aptly label the OFC "the gateway between inter-personal connection and internal balance."[19] Fortunately, we are able to continue to develop this part of the brain throughout our lives to make up for any childhood deficits. For example, we can learn ways of calming ourselves when we're upset, rather than acting out our anger. We can also become more socially astute and better able to recognize and respond to the emotions of others.

The OFC is also involved in regulating our autonomic nervous system (ANS), which adjusts our respiration rate, heart rate, perspi-ration, sexual arousal, and digestive processes. It is believed that the OFC monitors and activates the two parts of the ANS to maintain a healthy balance—the excitatory sympathetic nervous system, which is activated to respond to perceived danger through the fight or flight response, and the inhibitory parasympathetic system, which main-tains vital restorative functions while the body is in a state of "rest and digest."

Siegel and Hartzell also go on to explain other functions of the OFC.

> The orbitofrontal cortex also has to do with response flexibility, the ability to take in data, think about it, consider various options for responding, and then produce an appropriate response. Finally, it is believed that the orbitofrontal cortex is essential for the human creation of self-awareness and autobiographical memory.[20]

Another part of the higher brain that works together with the OFC to coordinate our minds and bodies and direct our attention is the anterior cingulate. Working in tandem with the OFC, the anterior cingulate plays a key role in integrating the emotional and cognitive components in brain functioning.

Let's look at a simplified example of how these parts of the brain work in tandem. Imagine you are on a beach vacation and go for a swim in the ocean. But you recently had a near-drowning experience, so the physical sensation of swimming in the ocean triggers your limbic system to recall that event and the feelings of terror associated with it. Your limbic system signals the OFC that you may be in danger as your reptilian brain increases your heart rate and respiration rate in preparation for dealing with a potential crisis. The OFC conveys this "danger alert" message to your cerebral cortex, where incoming sensory data along with knowledge of past experiences is used to make a logical determination that this is a false alarm. As this signal is conveyed via your OFC to your limbic system and reptilian brain, the danger signal is deactivated. And to think, all of this happens within a mere millisecond!

Left- and Right-Hemisphere Modes of Processing

The cerebral cortex is divided into left and right hemispheres connected by a dense band of fibers, called the *corpus callosum*, that transmit up to five billion signals between the two sides every second.[21] In 1981, neuroscientist Roger Sperry received the Nobel Prize for his research with individuals who had had their corpus callosum severed to treat epileptic seizures. Sperry's research demonstrated that the two hemi-spheres of the brain actually specialize in different modes of perception and information processing. In one experiment, subjects were seated at a table and instructed to reach under a screen to select common objects by touch rather than by sight. By flashing words to the far corners of the right or left visual fields, Sperry was able to send messages to either the left or right hemisphere of the patient's brain. When images were flashed to the left hemisphere, the subjects were able to reach for those objects under the screen and correctly identify them using language. When images were flashed to the right hemisphere, although patients found the correct items with their left hands, they were not consciously aware of having done so, and when asked, denied having seen an image or having grasped an item.[22] These subjects demonstrated that we can engage in intelligent behavior that is beyond our conscious awareness!

Sperry's work taught us a great deal about the differences between the left and right hemispheres of our brain. While both sides of our cortex are integrally interconnected and work in tandem, each part specializes in alternate ways of perceiving and processing incoming data. Although it is a vast oversimplification to say that we have separate left and right brains, we *can* say that the left side of the cortex seems to be predominantly active in using a logical, language-based, sequential processing mode. It uses words, numbers, and step-by-step reasoning to solve complex problems, and excels at recognizing cause and effect relationships. The right side of the cortex is predominantly involved in holistic, nonverbal, nonlinear processing of data. It uses symbols, metaphors, whole pictures or images, art, movement, bodily sensations, intuitive hunches, and feelings as its primary communication mode rather than language. It is invaluable for reading nonverbal social cues and for deriving new solutions to old problems through sudden insight and awareness. Rather than thinking in a step-by-step fashion, this is the part of us that grasps the whole of a situation or provides a sudden insight that opens up brand new, unseen potentials. While the left side of the brain specializes in what we often consider *thinking*, the right side of the brain accesses a deeper sense of *knowing* that transcends language and rational thought, and emerges from our inner Self.

Trauma and the Brain

Our brains are specially equipped to help us cope with events that can turn our lives upside-down—the unexpected death of a parent or child; the crippling car accident, the brutal sexual assault; the loss of our beloved home to a devouring forest fire. What happens in the brain when we experience stressful life experiences? When the limbic system registers a situation that is perceived as a potential threat to one's survival, the amygdala takes charge and floods the brain with stress hormones and neurotransmitters to cope with imminent danger. Since the brain has determined that this is a time to act rather than analyze, these chemicals temporarily override the prefrontal cortex's ability to employ rational analysis and problem solving in the moment. Once the danger has passed, the brain resumes normal functioning, and the individual has the opportunity to process the event and the thoughts and feelings associated with it, ultimately recording it as a sequential and integrated memory in the hippocampus.

But what of those events that exceed a person's capacity to cope due to their being prolonged, extreme, or repetitive? When a life experience or series of life experiences are more than we can take—when our system of coping is on overload—we call it a *trauma*. Our brain handles these situations differently in order to help us deal with the unthinkable.

> When we can't consciously come to terms with a
> potentially traumatizing event—by acknowledging,
> "That happened in the past, but I'm okay now"—then
> our brain protects us from further overwhelm by isolating
> the memories of the event in a "trauma capsule" buried
> in implicit memory, no longer connected with the brain's
> conscious processing of the experience or with other
> memories or learning that could help us cope.[23]

15

Such memories are stored in the amygdala as fragments of perception, emotion, and somatic experience, which lack the verbal context, meaningful associations, and greater perspective necessary to make sense of them. Traumatic memory gets locked in the midbrain region, the seat of perception, emotion, and motivation, where it may continue to trigger strong emotions, flashbacks, and heightened body states, without the person's conscious understanding of what is happening or why.[24] What's more, the traumatized brain gets stuck in a default cycle of extreme arousal followed by a frozen state of numbness and disconnection. At the same time, our logical, verbal brain centers and the parts of the brain that perform an integrative function are, in effect, locked out and incapable of helping to process the traumatic memory. The result of unresolved trauma is a short-circuited, disconnected brain. Where the brain's three regions normally function as a unified whole, the traumatized brain is fragmented, lacks integration, and continues to ignite neural pathways that create great distress for the person who's suffered the trauma.

Individuals with a short-circuited, disconnected brain are likely to be flooded with emotions without the mediating influence of the OFC and anterior cingulate to determine if the present situation is, indeed, a threatening one. They are likely to misread ordinary situations as dangerous or threatening, and react automatically without considering the context, entertaining options, and choosing the most appropriate response for the moment. These individuals typically feel as if they have no control over the powerful emotions that have overtaken them—seemingly out of the blue. What's more, the emotions they experience tend to be far more intense than the situation warrants. The war veteran hears fireworks and his implicit memory banks immediately draw the unconscious association with gunfire and flood him with feelings of terror, rage, despair, and powerlessness as he dives to the floor. The rape survivor smells the cologne on a man standing next to her on the bus—a smell she unconsciously associates with the rapist—and she is suddenly fearful, nauseous, and desperate to escape, without understanding why she feels this way. The man who endured brutal childhood beatings from his alcoholic stepfather finds himself consumed with rage and begins driving erratically when another driver cuts him off. The professional woman who was abandoned as a child collapses in despair as her husband departs for a week-long business trip.

Unresolved Emotions Keep Us Tethered to the Past

This triggering of overwhelming, out-of-control emotions that seemingly arise from nowhere is one of the key signs that we are under the spell of our traumatic past. It is important to keep in mind that we do not necessarily become spellbound when we have survived a traumatic event. Rather, we are only likely to be spellbound when we *still have unresolved emotions* concerning the event in question. We know we have made peace with our past when we can recall a particular traumatic event without having it trigger a strong emotional reaction.

Sometimes we do not take emotional baggage with us following a stressful life event. Or, we may leave with such baggage, but we later take advantage of life's opportunities to unload it. And sometimes we think we have no emotional baggage because we have locked it away, only to have life remind us of its presence many years down the road. It doesn't matter how long we have been carrying that baggage—there is always the opportunity to set it down once and for all and lighten our burden.

I have worked with scores of psychotherapy clients using the processes presented in this book, After using these methods, I typically ask my clients, "How are you feeling right now?" Interestingly, each and every one of them has always responded by saying the same thing: "Lighter." When we release the emotions that we have been carrying concerning our past, we are, indeed, lightening our load as we add light to those previously dark spaces within.

Brain Integration Fosters Healing

How do we sever the negative hold that the past has on us, awaken from our spellbound state, and reset our maladaptive default mode? By *integrating* our three brain regions and our two cerebral hemispheres! The challenge here is that we cannot accomplish this integration using rational thought and words. While our left hemisphere's analytical abilities combined with its verbal skills can be invaluable in helping us change under many circumstances, when it comes to working with trauma these abilities are of little or no use. Any efforts to work through the trauma using *only* language and logic are not only fruitless, but they are also likely to trigger a stress response rather than eliminate one.[25] In other words, we cannot talk through or reason away our default mode responses, and attempting to do so can even intensify our level of distress.

Similarly, our negative mental models do not change simply because we tell ourselves that they are illogical or false. For example, many clients tell me that they realize that they are worthy in their heads, but that they still feel unworthy deep within (indicating their chests). It is this dichotomy that we must find a way to bridge in order to heal. Logical arguments don't work for this purpose.

So—what does work? How do we heal nonverbal memories and their accompanying emotions and schemas, which are locked in the amygdala? Fortunately, the right side of the cortex has a direct line to the limbic brain. What's more, the limbic system can "hear" and "speak" the emotional, imagery-based, sensation-focused language of the brain's right hemisphere, and it is in a keen, nonverbal listening mode as a result of the biochemical effects that have impaired the functioning of the brain's neocortex.[26]

To awaken from our spellbound states we need to engage our right hemisphere in ways that may include working with imagery, symbols, metaphors, stories, movement, art, writing, music, emotions, and multisensory and somatic processing. This is the key that unlocks trauma that has been isolated in the lower brain centers, thus allowing us to recast our mental models and retire negative, self-limiting ways of behaving.

Over the past decades, I have seen numerous clients successfully utilize powerful, right-brain methods to birth a new Self. These approaches reach beyond conscious, logical thought to a realm that offers profound wisdom; deeply transformative experiences; and new, heightened awareness. In particular, I have found that guided imagery opens pathways of integration and healing that were previously blocked to those experiencing spellbound states. It is as if the light goes on, and they are able to peer into previously dark and frightening spaces with astounding clarity and remarkable insight. The next chapter addresses the healing power of imagery and provides guidance in how to begin to utilize imagery to reset your default mode. Then, in the chapters that follow, you will find additional exercises, using imagery and other tools, which will help engage right-hemisphere modes of processing to welcome a *new you* into existence.

Activating the Healing
Power of Imagery

One of the most powerful ways to activate healing, ignite integrative neural pathways, reset our brains' default-functioning mode, and attain states of mental and physical well-being is through the use of guided imagery. Imagery is surprisingly gentle and easy to use, considering the remarkable results it produces. As indicated in the last chapter, imagery provides a means of communicating directly with the older brain regions that specialize in emotion, motivation, and sensation and of engaging these centers in processing trauma that has been locked in the brain. As we repeat imagery processes that foster inner peace and relaxation, clear thinking and thoughtful action, new brain connections are established that dial down arousal levels and promote balance and integration in mind and body. The more we practice these imagery exercises, the more the new brain pathways become ingrained; eventually, these new neural circuits become the brain's default-functioning mode. This means a brain that has been wired for anxiety learns to be more peaceful; one that has been quick to anger becomes more steady and reasoned; one that has been on hyperalert learns to instead assess each new situation from a place of inner calm, confidence, and clarity.

Imagery Produces Remarkable Results

Guided imagery provides a means of identifying, and then reprogramming, faulty mental models that have been encoded in the nonverbal parts of our brain. These schemas exist beyond our conscious awareness, can be difficult to identify, and tend to remain impervious to reasoned arguments that they are illogical or untrue. Yet, with the use of the right-brain mode of processing, we can more easily pinpoint those negative mental models that hold us spellbound and rewire our thinking to accentuate alternate positive and life-affirming schemas.

Certain guided imagery processes work extremely well for releasing the past, changing negative schemas to positive ones, and deactivating the emotional charge that certain life events still hold for us. I have used these with countless clients, always with positive results; they work quickly and they evoke lasting changes. Imagery interrupts our automatic, default mode reactions and allows our brains to entertain new perspectives, formulate alternate responses, and make wiser choices by integrating and regaining access to all three brain regions and both hemisphere of the cortex. Implicit memories are processed with the assistance of the hippocampus and neocortex so that we are able to view them in context, derive new meaning from the experiences, and encode them as autobiographical memories. New synapses are formed which activate higher brain regions during situations that would otherwise have triggered automatic, unconscious reactions. The result is an increased ability to exercise wisdom, demonstrate self-control, and make choices in accordance with our highest intentions.

So often, our analytical selves are in a defensive posture from so many years of disappointment and despair. As a way of protecting the self from further discouraging outcomes, this part of us can be only too willing to discount or devalue our efforts to heal. Yet—it is only when we are willing to suspend disbelief that we open ourselves to the possibility of real change. By circumventing the linear, logical, mind, healing imagery can saturate the psyche and work its powerful magic without the dampening effect of worry, despair, hopelessness, fear, or doubt.

There has been much research proving the effectiveness of guided imagery. According to Belleruth Naparstek, a psychotherapist and expert in the use of guided imagery, there is evidence that imagery can be used to lower levels of anxiety and depression, improve our short-term immune system functioning, reduce pain due to arthritis and fibromyalgia, improve the hemoglobin A1C levels of diabetics, reduce binging and purging in bulimics, and increase the likelihood that infertile couples will conceive. Naparstek concludes, "Indeed, given the last twenty years of research findings from various clinical trials, it is surprising that imagery isn't prescribed as a universal, low cost, preventive health tool, in much the way that aspirin is used to reduce the likelihood of future heart attack and stroke.[1]

I've witnessed many remarkable results in clients regarding the ways in which they have benefitted from the use of imagery. Two of them stand out in particular. One was the case of a forty-five-year-old mother of two adult daughters. She had been sexually abused by her grandfather from the age of eight until she was sixteen. Valerie was highly anxious, deeply unhappy, devoid of confidence, and felt stuck working at a job she hated. Over the course of a year, we met once a month for psychotherapy sessions in which I utilized guided imagery and many of the exercises presented in this book as the primary mode of treatment. Toward the end of our work together, Valerie reported that, in addition to reducing her anxiety levels, gaining confidence, and landing a new job she loved, she had grown breasts for the first time in her life! It appears that awakening from her spellbound state through the use of imagery enabled her body to complete the physical development that had been temporarily obstructed by the sexual abuse she endured.

The second case involved another woman, Silvia, who was quickly losing her vision due to complications from diabetes. By the time she began to come periodically for psychotherapy, she had surrendered her driver's license due to blindness, and her ophthalmologist had told her that there was nothing more that could be done for her. Silvia loved guided imagery and listened daily to the recordings I made for her during our sessions. Over time, she was prompted from within to seek a second opinion from a specialist who was using an experimental form of eye surgery with diabetic clients. The specialist told Sylvia her chances of regaining her vision were very slim; however, he was willing to operate if she chose that intervention. Sylvia felt strongly guided to undergo the surgery, and she continued to use imagery before and after her operation. To the utter astonishment of her eye surgeon, her vision was greatly restored; after the procedure, Sylvia was able to read a size twelve font on her computer without the assistance of corrective lenses!

These two clients had certain key factors in common. They were both highly responsive to guided imagery and found that method was especially to their liking. Furthermore, each was dedicated to listening often to guided imagery recordings.

Numerous other clients have also reported that imagery has helped them overcome old patterns that were highly distressful. Imagery seems to be especially effective in helping individuals with sleep disturbances to train their brains to fall asleep and stay asleep. One woman listened nightly at bedtime to a guided imagery recording I made for her. After a year of using the recording to fall asleep, she told me that she had yet to hear the end of the recording! She vowed to listen to it while sitting up during the daytime so she could finally hear what I said to her in the final moments of the guided imagery. I have also used this approach to help anxiety-ridden individuals learn to attain and maintain inner calm, to assist clients with pain control, and to help others replace unhealthy habits with new behaviors.

Interestingly, I have had several women listen to my guided imagery recordings throughout their pregnancies. After the women gave birth, every one of them have reported that the guided imagery recordings have been very effective in calming their fussy or upset newborns and lulling them to sleep. Perhaps the babies recognize my voice from the womb and associate it with the relaxing sensations their mothers experienced while using these processes to feel more calm and comfortable during pregnancy.

Many clients have also reported that their cats (and sometimes dogs) seem very fond of the peaceful energy that is generated during imagery sessions and generally choose to be curled up where they can be in physical contact with their "person" while sessions are in progress.

Imagery Opens You to Another Dimension of Self

When you close your eyes and allow yourself to journey within, you can awaken to a whole new dimension of yourself. This dimension transcends space and time, and knows no limitation. By aligning with the *you* who resides on the inner plane, you can experience profound peace, higher wisdom, deep compassion, renewed confidence and courage, and an inspired, clear vision of yourself and the unlimited possibilities open to you in this lifetime. You can see the big picture of your life and receive guidance regarding the path of your highest good. And you can create changes in how you think, feel, and behave, with ease and joy.

Imagery serves as a bridge between our conscious and unconscious minds. It transports us to a vast, unconscious level of our being that has access to our innermost mysteries and greatest truths. This deeper Self has the capacity to help us change our thoughts, feelings, and behavior without struggle, to improve our physical well-being, and to open us to our greater creative potential. Using symbols, metaphors, and stories, guided imagery affords us the opportunity to become well acquainted with this deeper dimension of self and to benefit from its guidance, support, and love.

You are free to make whatever meaning you wish of these kinds of experiences. Some believe they are connecting with a form of source energy, their soul or spirit, or a spark of divinity within. Others believe they are making contact with a deeper and wiser part of themselves. Guided imagery is permissive in many respects. It does not require that you hold any particular spiritual or religious beliefs, and it is compatible with a belief in God or some kind of higher power. Imagery may, at times, open us to a transcendent space where we find ourselves communing with "helpers." You may see these as angels, guides, loved ones who have passed on, spirit animals, or anything you wish. Your experiences in guided imagery, often transcending words, are there for you to interpret or understand in your own unique way. You are the expert in your own imagery, as in your own life.

Often the metaphors and symbols that present themselves during guided imagery have powerful, transformative meanings for us. For example, a man was so inspired by the picture of a mountain he saw during a guided imagery session that he later ascended to the summit of Mount Rainier—his first mountain climbing expedition. One woman derived great personal strength and courage from the image of a mama grizzly bear. Another found that the picture of a huge ball of knotted rope provided her new insight into the nature of a particular relationship that was causing her distress. The symbols we evoke can ignite healing, inspire change, and activate new healing pathways in our brains and in our lives.

Guided Imagery Tips

The best part of guided imagery is that it is easy, fun, free or very low cost, and anyone can do it. All it takes is a willingness to close your eyes and use your imagination. Like anything, the more you do it, the more natural it will become for you, and the more you will benefit from its many positive effects.

Sometimes people ask if guided imagery is appropriate for children or adolescents, and my answer is, "Yes, absolutely." It helps if the language and concepts used are appropriate to the child's age level. And children's imaginary journeys are most effective if we make them shorter than those for adults.[2]

Adolescents may initially balk at the notion, but I have heard from a teacher at a juvenile hall that his students responded well to a group exercise listening to a guided imagery process. As with adults, adolescents seem to respond favorably to imagery that is meant to help them meet their personal goals, such as the desire to excel in tennis, pass an algebra class, or perform well in tryouts for the drill team.

If you are ever uncomfortable during an imagery process, and you don't want to continue, then feel free to stop. Always know that you are the one in control of this process. Trust yourself—you are in charge of your own healing. You will be guided from within concerning what is right for you. No one else knows better than you what you need. You are the expert when it comes to you!

For this process and others that follow in later chapters, you can either memorize each exercise beforehand, have someone read it to you very slowly, or record yourself reading it slowly so you can then play it back to do the exercise. You may wish to play relaxing music in the background while you go through the process. I like using music during my own imagery sessions and also for my clients. Any music used should be slow and soothing, allowing you to breathe deeply and feel calm and relaxed. I prefer music with simple, repetitive themes that are not intrusive but add depth and beauty to the experience. Often music helps us to better access our emotions during an imagery session; this can be very helpful for certain kinds of processing work.

When you are doing the guided imagery exercises, it is helpful to be playful with your imagination and to be willing to *pretend*. There is no one right way to use your imagination. Invoke as many of your senses as you can in your mental imagery and don't be concerned if you don't get a clear picture. Some people see things clearly when using their imaginations, while others feel, smell, hear, or just sense things. Again, there is no right or wrong way to do this. Whatever you experience is perfect. Do not worry if it doesn't feel like anything is happening as you are doing an imagery exercise. Just by being willing to try to quiet your mind and take this inner journey you are creating changes deep within you that will reveal themselves in time.

There may be a little voice in the back of your head during the guided imagery telling you that you are not doing it correctly. The voice may also try to distract you by reminding you of all the things on your to-do list. You can use that voice as a signal to refocus on the imagery. Continue to gently bring your attention back to the imagery as often as is necessary. Eventually the voice will go away.

For each imagery exercise, find a comfortable place where you can be alone, quiet, and uninterrupted for a period of time. The following process will require around fifteen minutes—others in this book may take as long as thirty or forty-five minutes. Choose a position (sitting or lying down) that allows you to keep your spine straight and to relax without falling asleep. It is a good idea to always do your imagery work in the same place—this helps to create familiarity and deepen the experience. Remember: the more you practice using guided imagery, the easier it will become, and the greater the results you will attain.

KEEP A JOURNAL

As you embark on this new healing pathway to greater joy, fulfillment, and well-being, I recommend that you keep a journal. You can use this to do some of the written exercises in this book and to record your dreams (which may provide you with additional answers as you work with your intuitive right-brain processes). I also suggest that you take some time after each guided imagery process to record your experiences.

EXERCISE 1 CREATING YOUR HEART SANCTUARY

The following guided imagery, will help you access deep states of inner peace and relaxation. This process is also used as a starting point in many of the other guided imageries you will find throughout this book.

1. Close your eyes and begin taking long, slow, deep breaths. Allow yourself plenty of time for every breath. Notice the rising and falling in the area below your navel as you inhale and exhale. Keeping your eyes closed, you may gently roll your eyes upward if it is comfortable for you. For some, this enhances the process of relaxation. Imagine that you are inhaling peace up through the soles of your feet. Every time you exhale, feel yourself letting go of all tension, just letting it drain away. Take all the time you need to feel more and more calm and comfortable. Breathe relaxation into any part of your body that needs to relax more deeply and completely. Feel your body responding by becoming more and more relaxed, surrendering to the serenity and comfort of this moment. Notice your mind becoming as calm and clear as a deep, blue sky on a cloudless summer day. Give yourself permission to take this minivacation as you begin to access the deepest and most peaceful part of your being.

2. Now imagine that the area around your heart is easily opening up and expanding until you become aware of a special

doorway. The doorway leads directly into your heart sanctuary—a place that is completely safe, peaceful, nurturing, and loving. It may resemble a favorite place you visited in the past, or someplace you have just created. In this setting, you can access your unlimited potential for creativity, inner guidance, self-transformation, and self-healing. Everything about your heart sanctuary is exactly as you want it to be. Use all your senses to imagine exactly how it looks, smells, feels, tastes, and sounds here in your heart sanctuary. Perhaps you are in a mountain meadow surrounded by towering pines where you detect the sweet smell of newly blossomed wildflowers permeating the air along with the fresh, musky sent of rich earth that comes after a gentle spring rain. Or perhaps you are strolling along a pristine beach and catch the scent of salt as the air blows softly against your skin, and the sun caresses you with its soothing warmth. This is your heart sanctuary, and you can create it exactly to your liking. Notice the intense colors and interesting textures. How many shades of green do you see? How does it smell? Is the temperature cool or warm, moist or dry? Do you hear music, a babbling brook, the sound of birds singing, or the leaves rustling in the wind? Notice that the air you breathe here is composed of tiny droplets of peace. Feel every level of your being becoming saturated with the serenity and love that are so abundantly available here. Drink it in and allow it to nurture every cell of your being. Notice how safe you feel, how completely supported, how calm and peaceful.

3. Spend as much time as you like exploring your heart sanctuary. Become aware of how good you feel just being here—safe and serene, calm and comfortable, peaceful and protected.

4. When you are ready to return to the room, tell yourself that you are coming back feeling clearheaded, refreshed, and alert. Open your eyes, stretch, and feel yourself returning fully and completely to the present moment.

You will often be asked to return to your heart sanctuary as a starting point for future exercises in this book. Practice visiting your
heart sanctuary daily, until you can easily and effortlessly imagine
yourself there.

What Did You Experience?

- What was it like for you to visit your heart sanctuary?
- What did you notice about the experience?
- Were there any surprises?
- What imagery was the most helpful for you in inducing
  a state of relaxation?
- Write down anything that occurred to you during the
  exercise that you want to be sure to remember.

✦

Saturate Your Brain with Peace

One of the most important things you can do for your brain is to
practice being peaceful as often as possible. Inner calm is the antidote
to stress—and we know that consistently high stress levels take their
toll on many of our bodily processes, making us more susceptible to
a host of diseases and aging us well before our time. When you are at
peace within, both your body and mind are able to function optimally.
Every moment you spend being peaceful fosters brain integration by
reducing arousal levels in the amygdala and other parts of the limbic
system so that all three brain regions can function in a coordinated
fashion to maintain well-being throughout your system. Research
using functional MRIs with subjects who are evoking imagery to relax
has revealed that the various parts of the cortex that process seeing,
hearing, smelling, and touching, respond when you are just *imagining*
doing these things. As you spend time in your heart sanctuary (as you
just did in the previous exercise), increasing amounts of your cortex
become involved and are able to communicate to your lower brain
centers that it is okay to relax deeply.[3] Practice in relaxing body, mind,

and spirit also rewires our neuronal networks so that inner peace and calm eventually become our new norm.

When you are feeling tranquil, you are most attuned to your inner wisdom. It is from a place of deep calm that you can hear the still, quiet voice of your deepest truth. Like a radio adjusted to eliminate static, serenity brings clarity to the broadcast of your inner guidance.

A peaceful state is healthy for your body. During periods of rest and inner calm, you press the off button on the body's stress reaction; your body relishes deep relaxation as a way of revitalizing itself. When you maintain a state of calm, you give your cells an opportunity to restore themselves to optimal functioning levels; while stress ultimately weakens your immune system, a peaceful state provides the ideal conditions for its strengthening and rejuvenation.

Many of us spend our lives in a state of constant turmoil, waiting for situations outside ourselves to change so that we can finally feel peaceful. The problem with this approach is that there will always be situations around us that will stress us if we allow them to. Our power lies not in controlling the situations, people, or events in our lives, but in controlling our *reactions* to them. Though it is a challenge to remain at peace in the midst of a busy and demanding life, you can learn to spend increasing amounts of time feeling calm and serene. It helps to have a gentle way of reminding yourself to relax when you catch yourself becoming uptight. Whenever you notice yourself feeling anxious, fearful, or upset, take a few slow, deep breaths and say to yourself: "I choose peace instead of this."

A good way to make sure you are breathing deeply is to first exhale forcefully and completely. The next inhalation will be a deep breath. It will feel as if your abdomen (below your navel) is a balloon being filled with air. As you exhale, you will notice your abdomen flattening.

With practice, you can train yourself to remember to choose peace when you would normally feel distress. Make an agreement with yourself to use certain signals throughout the day as a reminder to take some deep breaths and choose peace. For example, you can decide to take a deep breath and say "I choose peace instead of this" every time you hear the phone ring, or before making a phone call. Practice when you are driving in heavy traffic or are late for an appointment. Remind yourself to breathe deeply and choose peace when your children are squabbling or when you are opening your bills. Let each of life's little challenges be an opportunity to demonstrate your commitment to inviting greater serenity into your life.

Employing
Mental Rehearsal

When Dr. Milton Erickson was seventeen years old, he contracted polio, which left him unable to move anything except his eyes. He discovered that if he focused his attention and imagination on a particular body part, such as his right index finger, recalling what it had felt like to move that finger, over time he was able to feel a slight twitch take place in that muscle. This indicated to him that his brain was relearning how to move it. He continued to use focused attention and imagery until he was voluntarily able to move that muscle, and then used the same process with the other muscles throughout his body. Dr. Erickson was eventually able to retrain his body to move all its muscles. Next, he taught himself to walk again by mimicking his baby sister, who was learning to walk at the time. Within two years, he had recovered enough to take a canoe trip on his own down the Mississippi River.

Milton Erickson went on to become a physician and one of the world's most famous psychotherapists and hypnotherapists, utilizing what he had learned while paralyzed with polio. He understood the power of using mental imagery for stimulating physical and behavioral changes—something neuropsychologists have now documented in research using brain scans and other advanced technology. In a remarkable study led by Alvaro Pascual-Leone, researchers were able to document the effectiveness of mental imagery for developing and expanding new neural networks.[1] The first experiment involved three groups of voluntary subjects. The first group was instructed in how to play a simple five-finger sequence on the piano with one hand, which they then practiced for two hours every day for five days. The second group was not given any instruction, and were not aware of any specific sequence of notes to practice on the piano; they practiced or played whatever they wanted on the piano for two hours every day for five days. The third control group did not learn or practice anything during the experiment. When the area of the cortex involved with the motor activity of the hand was measured, it was found that the first group showed significant development and expansion of neural networks in this region of the brain. The second group showed similar, but only slight changes in the same brain region, while the third group showed no changes.

In the second experiment, a group of subjects watched what was taught to the first group, until they memorized the sequence without ever touching the piano. This group practiced the one-hand sequence *in their minds only* for two hours every day for five days. Researchers concluded that "mental practice alone led to the same plastic changes in the motor system as those occurring with the acquisition of the skill by repeated physical practice."[2] The mental practice group also demonstrated significant improvement in their ability to actually play the sequence on the piano, although significantly less than that demonstrated by the physical practice group. Researchers concluded:

> Mental practice alone seems to be sufficient to promote
> the modulation of neural circuits involved in the early
> stages of motor skill learning. This modulation not only
> results in marked performance improvement but also
> seems to place the subjects at an advantage for further
> skill learning with minimal physical practice.[3]

In other words, we can use mental rehearsal to train cells to fire together—and cells that fire together, wire together to form new neural circuits. It is by repeatedly stimulating the same communities of neurons that new neural networks develop and then become strengthened.

This is why the group that practiced anything they wanted on the piano did not demonstrate the same level of brain changes as those who used only imagery and never touched a keyboard.

It is interesting to note that the brain changes of the mental rehearsal group were in the exact same region of the brain as the changes for the physical practice group. This means we can use imagery to change our brains without physical practice—something Dr. Erickson discovered long before we had fMRIs and other measurement devices to track brain functioning. Incidentally, physical therapists are now experimenting with using imagery with stroke victims and the elderly who are too weak initially to do strength training to build their muscles. Clearly, these findings have far-reaching applications.

Mental rehearsal can also be used to stop old habits and replace them with new, healthier behaviors. Whatever it is you want to change in yourself or your life, mental rehearsal will help you get there more easily and quickly than if you simply try to push yourself or use willpower alone to alter your behavior. One reason for this is that *motivation follows imagination*. This means that if you imagine yourself doing something, after awhile you will find yourself increasingly motivated to engage in that behavior. Let's say you want to exercise more regularly, so you begin to picture yourself going to the gym and enjoying the feeling of working your muscles and benefitting from the terrific burst of energy and vitality that comes from a good workout. After practicing this imagery daily for several weeks, you are likely to find yourself motivated and inspired to do exactly what you have been envisioning. This is in direct contrast to using willpower alone to try to force yourself to go to the gym. When we use imagery, the desire to engage in the new behavior bubbles up from within us. Rather than fighting with ourselves, we feel an inner urge to change—a kind of drive that propels us in the direction of positive change.

You can use mental rehearsal to tap into your creative inspiration, to program yourself to respond differently in your relationships, and to find the courage and confidence to pursue your highest aspirations, stepping into a new way of being that expresses the fullness of who you are. This process enables you to establish a new mental map for where you are headed so that your brain and mind can assist you in finding the best pathway for reaching your desired destination.

How to Employ Mental Rehearsal

To use mental rehearsal, begin by identifying your goal or goals—that is, how you want to be different. When identifying your goals, it is important to focus on what you *want*, as opposed to what you *don't want*. For most of us, it is easier to say what we do not want in our lives than to be clear about what we want. Yet—this is an important step when one is using imagery to create changes.

When we are spellbound, we often find that the best way to cope is by not having desires. We become convinced that we can't or don't deserve to have what we want, and so we try to feel better by dousing the flames of our passions. After all, if you pretend you don't want something, it doesn't hurt so much when you don't have it. We practice thinking small and argue for our limitations. We adjust and accommodate to life's disappointments. And we stop believing that our situation will ever improve.

Yet, our deepest longings represent messages from our greater Self about our path of joy and fulfillment in this lifetime. When we ignore our desires, we prevent ourselves from living the rich and satisfying lives we were meant to live. We stunt our personal growth, and we choose suffering the status quo over risking an intoxicating ride on the powerful stream of well-being that flows through life.

Awakening from your spellbound state means becoming aware of your unlimited potential to do, be, and have whatever you desire in your life. It means beginning to direct the creative force within to consciously fashion the kind of life that thrills and delights you. You have the ability to stop surviving and start thriving. It all begins when you allow your desires to light the way for you.

WHAT DO YOU DESIRE?

Spend time asking yourself what it is you really want. How would you like yourself or your life to be different? You may wish for some form of material abundance, a life partner, perfect health, a different job, greater success in academics or sports, or perhaps something less tangible such as greater freedom, more fun, more loving relationships, inner peace, creative inspiration, youthful vitality, the ability to make a positive difference in the lives of others, or a deeper connection with your spiritual source. If you are not sure of what you want, you may desire greater clarity regarding what would make you happy, or clarity regarding the life path that would be in alignment with your higher purpose.

Do not censure yourself. Let go of thoughts that say it isn't possible to meet your goal; that you have never been able to be, do, or have it before; or that you haven't the slightest idea about how to go about attaining what you desire. Instead, allow yourself to be honest about identifying what it is you really desire, no matter how impossible it may seem or how hopeless you may feel about it.

FOCUS ON THE ESSENCE OF WHAT YOU WANT

As you formulate goals and begin to imagine what it is you want, it is best to focus on the *essence* of what you desire, rather than the *form*. For example, if you desire a new job, focus on the qualities you would like in your work environment, the kind of work you would like to be doing, the kinds of relationships you would like to have with your coworkers, and how you want to feel at work. Qualities you might specify may include that the job is stimulating and fulfilling; that you are doing something you love; that you are engaging your creative mind; that your work environment is friendly, supportive, attractive, and fun; or that you are well-compensated for your efforts. This is the essence of the new job. In contrast, avoid focusing on the *form*, such as working for a particular company in a particular building. When you want to create something very specific in your life—such as an intimate relationship with a particular person—it may trigger more fear and doubt than confidence as you imagine it. Because of this, it is better to imagine yourself in an intimate relationship that is ideal for you in every way, and to be open to the right person showing up at the right time in your life. If the person you are interested in is the right one for you, know that the relationship will unfold perfectly. In this way, you remain open to surprising, new possibilities coming into your life. Rather than limiting yourself, let your inner Self help you to find the right match for the essence of what you want. It will often be even better than anything you could have imagined.

It is also helpful to use imagery that you are familiar with and that is associated with your goals. When you use familiar imagery in your mental rehearsal, you build new neural networks more easily by connecting them to positive memories already encoded in your brain.

Why not take the opportunity right now to identify your goals and record them in your journal? Writing down your goals is one more way to activate your right brain's processing mode and so it is a powerful way to begin to program your brain for the changes you want to create in your life. The following exercise will help.

EXERCISE 2 IDENTIFYING YOUR GOALS

1. In your journal, describe how you would like yourself or your life to be different. These may be goals pertaining to anything that is important to you—health, relationships, work, home, school, athletics, creative endeavors, spiritual growth, and so on. State your goals in the present tense, as if they were already true. Write down what you want, using positive, present tense sentences. For example, write, "I *have* a wonderful life partner who adores me," rather than, "I *will* have a wonderful life partner who adores me," or "I'm not alone anymore." Try to identify the essence of what you are wanting. For example, "My body is healthy, strong, and brimming with vitality," or "I live fully and vibrantly in the present." List as many items as you would like. Remember that your goals are not written in stone, and you are free to alter, remove, or add to them any time you wish.

2. Once you have identified your goals, begin to think about and record past or present experiences, people, places, or things

that you associate with them. For example, if your goal is to have a body that is healthy, strong, and brimming with vitality, perhaps there was another time in your life when this is exactly how your body felt. Maybe you have a photo of yourself at that time, looking just the way you want to look now. Maybe you recall a specific place you visited when your body felt the way you want it to feel today, or remember what it felt like to move in that body. Perhaps you have seen a picture in a magazine that captures the look and feeling you are after in your new, healthy, strong, vibrant body. Maybe someone you know has the kind of body you would like to emulate. Find any images you can associate with your goal.

3. You may wish to create a collage that represents the goals you are intending by attaching pictures from cards or magazines to a poster board. Anything you can do to keep the images of what you want to attain front and center in your consciousness is a great way to begin reprogramming your brain for successful goal attainment.

Once you have completed steps one and two, you are ready to practice mental rehearsal. Find a time when you can spend twenty or thirty minutes without being interrupted. You may play soothing music in the background if you wish.

✦

EXERCISE 3 PRACTICING MENTAL REHEARSAL

1. Sit or lie down in a comfortable position. Make sure your spine is straight and your legs are uncrossed. Close your eyes and begin taking long, slow, deep breaths. Allow yourself plenty of time for every breath. Notice the rising and falling of the area below your navel as you inhale and exhale. Imagine that you are inhaling peace up through the soles of your

feet. Every time you exhale, feel yourself letting go of all tension—just letting it drain away. Take all the time you need to feel more and more calm and comfortable. You might imagine that you are surrounded by a beautiful cocoon of light. You might picture it as golden light or another color or colors, or just sense its presence around you. Experience the cocoon embracing you with safety, serenity, and love. Allow the light of that cocoon to be absorbed into each cell, spreading peace and relaxation, as if all your cells were producing a beautiful note in perfect harmony. Note that each cell absorbs just the amount it needs to be replenished and restored. Experience your body responding as it becomes more and more relaxed, surrendering to the serenity and comfort of this moment. Notice your mind becoming as calm and clear as a deep blue sky on a cloudless summer day as it, too, is saturated with peace. Give yourself permission to take this minivacation as you prepare to venture even more deeply within.

2. Now, imagine that the area around your heart is easily opening up and expanding until you become aware of a special doorway. The doorway leads directly into your heart sanctuary—a place that is completely safe, peaceful, nurturing, and loving. It may resemble a favorite place you visited in the past, or someplace you have just created. Fill in all the details exactly to your liking. Engage as many of your senses as you can. In this setting, you can access your unlimited potential for creativity, inner guidance, self-transformation, and self-healing. Everything about your heart sanctuary is exactly as you want it to be. Use all your senses now to imagine exactly how it looks, smells, feels, tastes, and sounds here in your heart sanctuary. Feel every level of your being becoming filled with the serenity and love that are so abundantly available here. Drink it in and allow it to nurture every cell of your being. Notice how safe you feel, how completely supported, how calm and peaceful.

3. In your heart sanctuary, you find a lovely spot in which to rest and drift into a comfortable sleep. While asleep, you begin to picture yourself as if the changes you want to create have already happened. Your movie is in the present tense. You are living the life you desire. You have attained your goals. Your dreams are now a reality. Imagine what that feels like. Engage all your senses. Make it as real as you can, embellish it, and have fun playing with your imagination. Allow yourself to get excited about it—to feel whatever emotions you associate with having accomplished your goals.

4. Slowly, begin to prepare yourself to awaken and return to the room. When you are ready to awaken completely, tell yourself that you are coming back, feeling clearheaded, refreshed, and alert. Open your eyes, stretch, and feel yourself returning fully and completely to the present moment.

Remember that it is important to practice mental rehearsal daily in order to create and strengthen the new neural networks through repetition.

What Did You Experience?
Take some time to record your experience in your journal.
*   What was it like for you to practice using mental rehearsal?
*   What did you notice about the experience?
*   Were there any surprises?
*   Write down anything that occurred to you during the exercise that you want to be sure to remember.

Start Dreaming about Getting What You Want

Continue to daydream about what your life will be like when your desires become a part of your reality. Be playful and lighthearted as you imagine and invent future stories in which you have and enjoy whatever it is you want. Put yourself in those scenes and imagine what it feels like to experience the fulfillment of your dreams. Get excited about what you envision. Make it as real as you can. Have fun conjuring up ever more pleasing episodes in your future life story.

Sadly, all too often, well-meaning parents and teachers who wanted to protect us from disappointment have discouraged us from visualizing our dreams. They have cautioned us to "face reality" and "get our heads out of the clouds," as if our flights of fancy were a personality defect that must be eradicated. In reality, everything we wish to attain in life begins in our imagination. We use our creative daydreaming to chart the course of our lives, prepare ourselves for the journey, recognize the signposts that point the way, and familiarize ourselves in advance with our destination. Imagining yourself being, doing, or having what you desire is the key that unlocks the door to making it happen.

Often, the life we want is in direct contrast to the life we are living. We want financial abundance, but we have an abundance of debt. We want freedom, but we feel imprisoned by our responsibilities. We want physical health and vitality, but we feel tired and weighted down. Beware of the message from your critical mind that says you can't significantly change your current reality: If you are poor, you will always be poor. If you are alone, you will always be alone. If you are in physical pain, you will never experience relief. Your negative thoughts may fortify their messages by pointing to other times when you tried to change yourself or your life and seemingly failed. The relapses. The personal and professional rejections. The unhappy relationships. Don't let these thoughts discourage you from believing in your power to create what you desire.

No matter what kind of life you are living today, it can be different tomorrow. You have already made significant changes in your life that have been positive and life affirming. Take a moment to write down all the changes, big and small, you have made for the better throughout your life. And then, remind yourself that you can do it again.

The key is to deal with the present-moment reality of your life, without becoming seduced into thinking this is all there is. Remember that your life is a journey, and this is just one brief stopping point along the way. For any aspect of your life that does not please you, focus on where you want to go next, instead of where you are or have been. Realize that there are unlimited possibilities stretching before you in every direction. If you end up choosing a route that doesn't bring you joy, you can always change your course.

THINK ABOUT WHY YOU WANT IT

Spend time thinking about how whatever you want will enrich your life and the lives of others, enabling you to cultivate higher qualities, such as love, wisdom, courage, joy, self-appreciation, generosity, and compassion. How will having what you desire make you a better person? In what ways will it enable you to grow? What do you hope to learn from the experience? How will it foster your spiritual development? Are there any ways in which you will be able to make the world a better place by creating what you desire? Focus on the ways in which the manifestation of your desires will be a source of personal evolution and enable you to bring more light to the world.

Begin demonstrating today the qualities that you are hoping to attain with the fulfillment of your desires. For example, if you think having a special relationship will make you a more loving person, find new ways to express more love today. If you believe that having a better job will make you feel happier and more secure, try to feel happier and more secure now. Perhaps you believe that having more money in the bank will enable you to feel more free and be more generous. Dare to feel more free and demonstrate greater generosity in this moment. If you think losing weight will help you to accept yourself, begin to think and act in a more self-accepting manner while at your present weight. Be the kind of person you hope to become when your dreams come true, and watch your life change for the better.

Harmonize Your Energy with Your Desires

Play with the image of achieving your goal until it feels perfectly natural and normal to have what you desire. Envision what it will be like to have what you want, until you and your desires are in perfect harmony. How do you know when you have accomplished this? When imagining yourself being, doing, or having what you want generates no uncomfortable feelings or reactions. No doubts, no anxiety, no fears, no frustration. You know you deserve to have it, and you can easily picture yourself having or attaining it. And, only positive feelings are associated with having your dreams come true.

A good way to identify what it feels like to be in harmony with what you want is to think of something positive that you easily allow into your life. It can be as simple as delicious food on your dinner plate or a hug from your best friend. When you think of this thing you easily accept, notice how you feel inside. Experience it fully, in all its emotional richness. Then, try to capture that same feeling when you think about whatever you want to create in your life.

HOLD YOUR DESIRES LIGHTLY

Imagine that you are at the beach and that you pick up a handful of sand. Notice that when you hold your palm in an open and outstretched manner, the sand remains, but the minute you close your hand into a fist, the sand slips through your fingers. The same is true of your desires. When you are open to receiving the fulfillment of your desires in whatever form they may come, you are most likely to realize your dreams. When you decide that you *must* have things a certain way, that you *need* to have things work out according to your specifications, you are holding your desires too tightly, and you are unlikely to realize their fulfillment. The more attached we become to a specific outcome or form, the more anxious we tend to be, and the more we are likely to feel fearful that things will not work out as we have decided they must. As stated earlier, anytime you continue to feel anxious, fearful, or desperate about a particular goal, it is best for you to make your goal more general. For example, perhaps you have decided that you want one, specific, career opportunity to work out for you. Soon thereafter, you notice that every time you focus on this goal, you become worried that things will not work out as you would like. This is a sign that you are holding this desire too tightly. Your best option would be to focus on opening to attract the job opportunity of your dreams, and trust that if the job you have focused on is meant to be yours, it will all work out perfectly. If not, then there is another opportunity that is even better waiting in the wings.

Tune Into and Follow Your Inner Guidance

Once you have begun to imagine what you want to create in your life, begin to follow any urges to take action which arise within you. It's as if you were on a treasure hunt, and the clues for which direction to go are offered to you, one by one, on the inner plane. At times, it may not be clear how following these inner urgings will lead you to your intended goal. Making a phone call, sending an e-mail, visiting a friend or relative, attending a class or workshop, joining a club, traveling to a new place, speaking to an interesting stranger, or reading a particular book may, to your surprise, take you one step closer to living out your dreams.

Your inner guidance will always lead you toward your intended destination. The messages from your deeper Self will be gentle nudges, rather than aggressive shoves in a particular direction. Whenever you feel yourself particularly motivated or inspired to do something, your inner Self is letting you know that you are on track. Do what makes you happy, and it will lead to the fulfillment of your fondest desires.

This is not to say that when we follow our addictive cravings, it is our inner Self guiding us to do so. Most of us recognize the difference between a craving for sugar, alcohol, or a relationship with a particular person, and the inspiration that moves us to play with our children, do a good deed, create something beautiful, or develop a project that makes the world a better place. An unhealthy craving feels like an intense, gripping, even desperate need that must be met quickly without concern for the outcome—such as when we feel compelled to binge on donuts beyond the point of fullness. In contrast, our inner guidance feels lighter, permissive, softer, and more gentle in its direction, generating a sense of inner peace and balance rather than one of urgency. For example, we may be inspired to prepare and savor a favorite meal out of love for our body and a desire to give it the nutrients it needs to stay healthy.

Focus on Little Successes

Pay attention to any changes, however small, that are moving you in the direction of your goal. Notice each little success, and more will follow. It is tempting to focus on how far we still must go on the journey toward our goal. But in focusing on what we have not yet accomplished, we end up feeling frustrated, hopeless, and discouraged. Change often happens in small increments, and the more we notice the little steps we take in the direction of where we want to go, the more successful we will be. For example, when I am writing a book, if I just focus on how many more pages I have yet to write, chances are I will become overwhelmed and even give up. By noting each time I write a paragraph or a page, I can feel a sense of accomplishment that helps me to continue to move forward. Although I may not sit down to write as often as I tell myself I "should" do so, I try to commend myself for the times that I do follow through on my plan to spend time writing.

In the next chapter, you will have the opportunity to learn more about how we become spellbound and to identify any reoccurring themes in your life that you intend to change.

Then, in future chapters, I will provide you with a step-by-step process for beginning to awaken from your spellbound state by using imagery to create new, healing pathways of neural integration.

4

Identifying
Spellbound Themes

As discussed in chapter 1, when we are spellbound, we tend to repeat the same negative patterns in our lives, under different circumstances but with the same unhappy outcomes. Our unconscious negative mental models, or maladaptive schemas, provide the blueprint for the kinds of self-sabotaging behaviors that are likely to be prevalent in our life story. Although some professionals refer to schemas as "core beliefs," I prefer to use the terms *schemas* and *mental models* because these perspectives are not formed at the conscious level. Hence, we tend to think of them much as we think of the earth's gravitational pull—as something we just know to be true about reality. We do not recognize that we have formed our schemas as a result of our early life experiences and that they have determined our default-functioning mode.

Maladaptive schemas and their corresponding spellbound themes are common among those who experienced abuse, neglect, loss, violence, hardship, natural disasters, emotional impoverishment, or physical deprivation, as well as among those who were overindulged, overprotected, or pampered in their early years. Not everyone with the same childhood experiences will end up spellbound or enact the same spellbound themes. Our temperaments and personalities play a central role in determining how we cope with painful or destructive life events.

Many psychologists have noted the tendency for humans to reenact their early traumas throughout their lives; Freud referred to this as the *repetition compulsion*. Until the emergence of the new brain science, we had limited understanding as to why someone would continue to replay painful childhood themes well into his or her adult years. We now understand that our memories of these events, and the emotions they evoke, are locked in the limbic system, along with the negative mental models associated with them. The brain's neural pathways for dealing with these life situations were established in our early years based upon our limited perspective at that time, and without the benefit of our higher mind's broader view and problem-solving capabilities. These brain circuits were designed to meet our need for survival as children, and they served that purpose well. In adulthood, our brains continue to utilize the same neural networks as their default mode, even though the consequences for doing so become increasingly painful and unsatisfying.

Spellbound Themes and the Law of Attraction

In recent years, there have been a number of popular books and movies that describe the law of attraction and the role it plays in our lives. The law of attraction is based on the notion that like attracts like—that what we send out into the world in the form of our energy is what we ultimately get back. According to this model, each of us emits a vibration, consisting of our thoughts and feelings on any given topic. This vibration determines what we attract into our lives. Often, we are not consciously aware of what our vibration is on a given topic, but by looking at the state of our lives, we can determine whether our vibration is working in our favor or needs an "adjustment."[1]

Because our vibration can be outside our conscious awareness, we can find ourselves attracting people and situations into our reality that are not at all in alignment with what we want. For example, if we want financial abundance but continue to feel that we do not deserve to have lots of money, or that it is not a possibility for us, and if we continue to focus on our current state of lack, then chances are that we will continue to attract more of the same. While we may desire abundance, our vibration is not in alignment with that desire. In order to attract what we want, we must change our deeper feelings about what we deserve, alter our expectations about what is possible for us, and then focus our thoughts on abundance rather than lack.

I mention the law of attraction here, not because this book is meant to argue in favor of or in opposition to this model. Rather, it can be helpful to look through the lens of the law of attraction when we consider how we repeat the spellbound themes in our lives: we emit certain vibrations we established in early childhood. These vibrations are comprised of the nonverbal mental models and emotions that have been encoded in our limbic system based upon our early traumatic experiences. The processes presented in the book for awakening from your spellbound state can be seen as processes for changing your vibration regarding central life themes that have to do with self-worth, relationships with others, and the world at large. According to the law of attraction, when we change our vibration, we change what we attract. And indeed, in my experience, those who use these exercises to awaken from their negative trances do stop attracting what they don't want and begin attracting what they do want into their lives.

You don't have to believe in the law of attraction for these methods to work. What this approach offers is simply another perspective to look at why your unresolved traumas and negative mental models may unconsciously contribute to the repetitive spellbound themes that you want to change. In liberating yourself from the past that holds you captive, you are altering your vibration in ways that open you to a world of new possibilities!

The Casting of the Spell

We become spellbound during the distressful moments of our lives when we experience an unpleasant or unbearable situation in which we are flooded with strong emotions that cannot be expressed. During these moments, we feel powerless, form maladaptive mental models, lose part of ourselves, and become fixated in our personal development. Let's examine how traumas initially activate spellbound states.

Since traumatic events are painful, frightening, and overwhelming, it is normal for them to activate a flood of intense, unpleasant feelings. During traumatizing events, we are deluged with a range of emotions, which may include shame, anger, terror, rage, guilt, hate, frustration, and grief. The overwhelming nature of these events triggers the release of hormones and neurotransmitters in our limbic system. This flooding cuts us off from the higher language centers of the brain and records these emotions in the nonverbal amygdala, which governs strong emotions such as anger and fear. What's more, the shocking nature of traumatic episodes may cause a psychological survival mechanism wherein we disconnect or disassociate from what is taking place. Thus, we become disconnected from parts ourselves during the event and periodically thereafter. While this is nature's coping mechanism (as discussed in chapter 1), it does not make the bad feelings go away—it makes it possible only for us to survive a tragedy without falling apart at the time. We may be fooled into thinking that our numbness means we don't have any strong feelings about the catastrophic event. But that numbness is only an anesthetic that protects us from pain that our subconscious feels may be too much to endure at the time. Some of us become addicted to such a psychological painkiller and go through decades of our lives numbing ourselves to any awareness of unresolved feelings.

Even if our brain did not block the expression of emotion during a traumatic episode, it may be unsafe to express feelings, as in the case of a child who is being abused by an adult. The child knows that saying how he or she feels means risking further harm. In some situations, it can even be life threatening for the victim to speak up. In addition, children rarely have the language to express what they are feeling during or after a painful and confusing incident. When given the opportunity to vent emotions, children often have difficulty expressing their feelings. At times, well-meaning adults may discourage a child from expressing negative feelings by saying things like "Be brave; don't cry," or "You shouldn't be afraid." Children may get the message that it is not okay for them to feel whatever they may be feeling. Some children also try to "protect" their caregivers by not speaking out about their experiences.

Intense, unexpressed emotions do not go away. They lie buried in the dark places within us. Until we make peace with our past, we may find ourselves in situations that activate those original feelings over and over again.

It is also natural for us to feel powerless during traumatic events. Whether we are confronted with a natural disaster, the death of a sibling, a criminal assault, or the wrath of a raging parent, we are generally in a helpless position to stop the dreaded event from taking place. Our frustration and suffering are intensified during such an ordeal because of our complete lack of control over what is happening to us or to those we love. We are left feeling vulnerable and incapable of protecting ourselves or others. Often, powerlessness and victimization become a central theme in our life script.

During original traumas, we are especially likely to develop maladaptive mental models about ourselves and our lives. For example, we may conclude that people we love will always hurt or leave us, or that the world is an unsafe place. It is common for children who are mistreated by their caregivers to blame themselves, resulting in the perspective that they are bad or unlovable and that they deserve to suffer. Throughout his childhood, Jason was routinely beaten by his father, who accompanied the beatings with reminders that Jason was a "stupid idiot who would never amount to anything." Like most abused children, Jason developed the maladaptive schema that he deserved the horrible beatings he received from his father, and that he is fundamentally bad, stupid, worthless, and unlovable. Jason absorbed his father's words, spoken in rage, and took them as the absolute truth about himself. As an adolescent, Jason became addicted to drugs and ended up in a juvenile detention facility. In adulthood, Jason is lonely, suicidal, and battles alcoholism. The mental model that he is bad and unworthy continues to play a central role in his life drama.

Each of us spends our early years establishing mental models about life in general and other people. For example, we note if others can be trusted, what our capabilities are, what our shortcomings are, and what we deserve in life. We formulate these schemas based on our life experiences, how we are treated, and what happens to us, as well as through observations we make about the important people in our lives and what we are taught by family members, teachers, and friends. These mental models lead to habitual ways of thinking that we often automatically revert to throughout our lives—unless we make a conscious effort to entertain different thoughts.

We use our mental models to formulate our expectations. Once we have decided to expect the worst, then it is only a matter of watching our negative drama unfold in just the way we have unwittingly set it up. Sadly, most of us consider our unfulfilling life experiences to be evidence that our negative expectations are indeed correct.

Our spellbound state blocks us from seeing the truth about ourselves and our life situations in three ways. First, our perception is distorted by filters that screen out positive input. Caitlin could not recognize or hear her husband's message that he loved and valued her. Another client, who really wanted to be in a relationship, was blind to a man's efforts to indicate he was interested in her. And Dean felt that he was poor and completely lacking in financial security, although his retirement account alone totaled over one million dollars.

Second, we tend to focus exclusively on the negative side of things and exaggerate it. Andrew hears five compliments and one small criticism, but he focuses exclusively on the critical comment, seeing it as a much bigger issue than was originally intended. Beatrice lost fifteen pounds and, rather than celebrating her accomplishment, she feels like a failure for not yet being at her ideal weight. Anna considers herself stupid because she did poorly in math, although she excelled in her language arts classes.

Third, we are likely to generalize from one negative experience to all other similar situations. Matthew, a talented actor, was rejected at one audition, so he assumes he will be rejected at all others. Denise's last boyfriend cheated on her and broke her heart; she now assumes that any man she meets will be unfaithful.

It is important to note that, while in a spellbound state, we are unaware of how our perceptions are being distorted. We don't even think to question the way things are, and believe that our interpretations of reality are the absolute truth. Not surprisingly, as we grow in conscious awareness, we are often amazed and even shocked to discover that things are not at all as we held them to be.

During traumatic episodes, we may also become disconnected from positive aspects of ourselves. It is not that these disconnected parts are gone forever, but we have temporarily lost the ability to access them. What are these missing parts? It depends upon the kind of trauma and the person who experiences it. Victims of sexual abuse may temporarily lose their ability to find pleasure in sexuality. Those who experience natural disasters like floods or hurricanes may misplace their sense of security and stability. Those who are the target of prejudice and discrimination may lose sight of their trust and faith in others. Depending upon the situation, we may lose touch with such qualities as courage, determination, the ability to love, playfulness, inner peace, or self-confidence. Naturally, it is also possible for us to find new inner resources during traumatic episodes. Sometimes it is through surviving such painful circumstances that we discover a previously hidden strength!

When we experience trauma, it is natural to do what we can to avoid suffering; this means calling up our psychological defenses. The problem is that while we are spellbound, we may continue to use the same coping strategies long after they have become counterproductive. Thus, in certain situations as adults, we may end up behaving in the same way we behaved when we were children—with disappointing results. Typically, the situations that trigger our childlike response pattern resemble the original trauma in some way. For example, when his boss would get angry with him, George reported that he felt like he was a bad little boy again, in danger of being yelled at by his raging mother. George's response to these situations was to feel terrified, say nothing in his own defense, and avoid being around his boss whenever possible. Not surprisingly, these were the same actions George took as a child to protect himself from his mother's wrath.

Josie was in a military family that frequently moved. After having to leave dear friends behind several times, Josie learned to protect herself from such losses by not letting anyone get too close to her. As an adult,

Josie is lonely and has few close relationships. The walls she erected as a child are still there, although the circumstances of her life have changed considerably. In her efforts to keep herself from experiencing the pain of loss, she has also shut out the joys of love and intimacy. Josie is not conscious of her walls and doesn't understand why she has such difficulty making friends. The spell she is under shrouds her in a fog, preventing her from recognizing the ways in which she perpetuates her loneliness.

Not everyone employs the same defensive tactics given the same stressful circumstances. People of different personality types often reveal a preference for utilizing different kinds of psychological protection. (If you're interested in learning more about the relationship between personality and defenses, read my book *Survival Games Personalities Play* in which I address this topic in detail.)

The Spellbound Template

Early traumas form the template for spellbound behavior. As you can see in the following chart, once we are spellbound, we continue to create and attract situations that resemble the original trauma, activating the same thoughts, feelings, and reactions.

During the initial trauma, a person will	experience strong emotions
	feel like a powerless victim
	form maladaptive mental models
	lose parts of the self
	employ coping strategies

A person who is spellbound will repeatedly	reexperience the same emotions
	feel powerless
	reinforce maladaptive mental models
	remain disconnected from parts of the self
	employ the same coping strategies

Charlotte's Spellbound Behavior

Charlotte was sexually abused by her father throughout her childhood and adolescence. As an adult, she finds herself attracted only to married men—often with the same first name as her father. Although she longs for a loving partnership, she engages in one painful affair after another. Let us examine Charlotte's spellbound behavior using the spellbound template.

Each time Charlotte has an affair with a married man, she feels the tremendous shame and self-disgust she originally felt when her father abused her. The secretive nature of each affair and fear of exposure are also familiar to her. Charlotte's father had threatened to kill her dog if she told anyone what he was doing to her.

Charlotte also revisits the experience of helplessness, hopelessness, and powerlessness she felt during her childhood abuse each time a male partner mistreats her. Thus, she continues to play the role of victim in her life story.

In addition, Charlotte's affairs remind her that she really is unlovable and unworthy, and that men she loves will always hurt her. While spellbound, she does not think to question the validity of the limiting attitudes and habitual thoughts that keep her imprisoned in her own unhappy existence.

Throughout the replaying of this painful scenario, Charlotte remains cut off from her powerful, capable, confident adult self, devoid of self-esteem and self-respect. Hence, the very qualities that Charlotte needs to maintain a satisfying intimate partnership seem inaccessible to her.

Charlotte reverts to feeling and behaving like a dependent and needy adolescent in response to her partner's actions. Though she is aware that her actions are not getting her what she really wants, she has been unable to break the pattern. She remains an abused teenage girl in a woman's body.

When Charlotte's father molested her, she learned to turn off her sexual feelings and physical sensations in order to survive those painful scenes. When engaging in sexual activities as an adult, Charlotte still finds that she becomes numb, and feels as though she is disconnected from her body. In each new relationship, she is disappointed when she is unable to feel physical pleasure during sex. Although the survival tactics of childhood are no longer necessary, she has yet to relinquish them in adulthood.

Although we have been focusing on Charlotte, it is also important to note that each of Charlotte's married boyfriends is probably grappling with his own unresolved past. It is common for those who are spellbound to be attracted to one another. And each is likely to behave in ways that revisit the other's most painful traumas. No doubt, in their affairs with Charlotte, these men are acting out their own spellbound template.

Common Spellbound Themes

Generally, one or two themes may be dominant in our lives, but there may be several others that also play key roles in our behavior. It may be difficult at first to recognize a spellbound theme that is playing itself out in your life. In some cases, you may feel ashamed and want to protect yourself from this awareness. It is also possible that you may be fearful of changing, or in some way want to cling to the drama that you know rather than opening yourself to something new and unknown.

The deeper, wiser part of you, however, knows if there is one or more of these themes that applies to you. Pay attention to your gut feelings as you read the list, as they will often provide clues about which of these themes is most prevalent in your life. If you do see yourself in any of these descriptions, be gentle with yourself. Remember, you developed this pattern because of your early life experiences, and it served you well at that time; however, your brain has been operating on automatic pilot ever since. Reading this book is a sign that you are looking to make a change—and that is what counts. Your life today is in your hands, and no matter what you have lived through, you have the power to change it more to your liking.

As you review common spellbound themes, it's good to remember that the purpose of exploring them is not to blame your parents or anyone else for your unhappiness. Chances are your caregivers were also under the spell of their past, and they did the best they could under the circumstances. This is not to say that what may have happened to you was okay—it is just to recognize that in many respects, your caregivers were operating unconsciously and repeating patterns they acquired themselves in childhood.

Exercise 4 lists thirteen common themes along with the schemas that are associated with them. As you work through the exercise, you may think of a theme that applies to you that is not listed here, as this list is not exhaustive.

Authors Jeffrey Young and Janet Klosko discuss eight of the following thirteen themes in their book *Reinventing Your Life*.[2] These are the themes of abandonment, mistrust, abuse, dependency, vulnerability, defectiveness, unrelenting standards, and entitlement. The authors emphasize that there are three ways that we may deal with our spellbound themes: by accepting them, avoiding them, or overcompensating for them.[3] When we accept our spellbound themes, we give in and give up—our attitude is one of painful acceptance and hopelessness. When we avoid our spellbound themes, we find ways of not feeling the pain associated with them. Addictions to food, drugs, alcohol, sex, pornography, television, video games, spending, or other such endeavors may be the result. Those of us who overcompensate for our spellbound themes try to mask deep feelings of insecurity and inadequacy by working hard at appearing successful, superior, or perfect.

EXERCISE 4 HOW MUCH DO YOU RELATE TO EACH SPELLBOUND THEME?

Following each description of the thirteen spellbound themes, you will see a one to ten scale where you can rate how much you identify with a particular schema. Circle the number that best applies to you. A score of zero indicates that you don't relate at all to a particular theme. This means you don't see it impacting you or your life in any way. A score of ten indicates you relate very much to a particular theme, and you see it playing a major role in your life.

Abandonment

People who relate to the spellbound theme of abandonment are forever fearful that loved ones will leave them—whether through death, finding someone else they would rather be with, or simply walking away. They may feel threatened by even the slightest amount of time spent apart from someone they love. Melinda, whom I described at the beginning of chapter 1, is an example of someone who replays this theme in her life. People whose lives reflect this theme often cling to those they love for fear of losing them and may demand lots of reassurance, or jealously accuse others of straying. As a result, the very things they do to try to hold on to those closest to them end up pushing them away, resulting in a cycle of abandonment. People under the spell of this theme either were overprotected in childhood or they experienced a lot of loss, upheaval, and instability in an unsafe and insecure home environment. This schema can be summed up with the statement: "People I love will always abandon me."

How much do you relate to this schema?

Abandonment (Schema: People I love always abandon me.)

0	1	2	3	4	5	6	7	8	9	10
NOT AT ALL										VERY MUCH

Mistrust

Often, early trauma involves other people who neglect or mistreat us in some way. And too often, those who abused or neglected us are the very people we completely depended upon for our survival—our parents and other caregivers. When this happens, we are prone to taking on the *mistrust* theme in life. After all, if you can't rely on those entrusted with your care, who can you trust? If you are acting out the mistrust theme, you do not trust others enough to allow them to get close. You may erect walls to isolate yourself from others and maintain plenty of emotional distance. You may push people who care for you away, by getting angry or abusive when they are loving, or provoke others until they finally do what you expect them to do—walk away without looking back. Another indication that you may relate to this theme is that you might insist on remaining highly independent—even in your marriage. Since you do not trust others to be there for you, it is safer to function on your own and never need anyone. Natalie, a twenty-five-year-old client, did not trust women and had never had a female friend. Natalie's mother had consistently betrayed her confidence in childhood by talking badly about Natalie behind her back, revealing Natalie's secrets to others, and making promises she would not keep. When Natalie told her mother that she had been sexually abused by a family member, Natalie's mother did nothing to protect her from further contact with the abuser and cautioned Natalie not to embarrass the family by telling anyone what had happened. This schema can be summed up as: "Other people cannot be trusted."

How much do you relate to this schema?
Mistrust (Schema: Other people cannot be trusted.)

0	1	2	3	4	5	6	7	8	9	10

NOT AT ALL   VERY MUCH

Undeserving

During early traumas, it is common for us to feel that we are to blame for whatever bad thing is happening to us. Children blame themselves, at some level, for the death of a family member, a car accident, or their parents' divorce. I have treated many men and women who were physically or sexually abused in childhood, and they all blame themselves for their abuse. I have even had clients who blame themselves for not having protected a brother or sister from being beaten by a drunken parent. When we blame ourselves for some horrible thing that befalls us or someone else, we ultimately decide we must be bad. And because we believe we are bad, we take on the *undeserving* life theme, which is associated with the feeling that we are not worthy of good things like love, joy, success, prosperity, good health, peace of mind, or a fulfilling life. We may want these things more than anything in the world; however, we do not allow ourselves to have them because we believe we are not good enough. For example, if you feel you are unworthy of love, you will make certain that you do not allow yourself to receive love in your life. Love can be knocking at your door, but you will either not hear it, or lock the door and run the other way. You may even unconsciously seek out relationships in which it is guaranteed that love is not part of the equation. This is because *we only allow ourselves to have what we feel we truly deserve in our lives.* This schema can be summed up as: "I am unworthy."

How much do you relate to this schema?
Undeserving (Schema: I am unworthy.)

0	1	2	3	4	5	6	7	8	9	10

NOT AT ALL   VERY MUCH

Abuse

People who were badly mistreated as children often continue to find themselves in situations where they are physically, verbally, or sexually abused. As they play out the *abuse* life theme in their adult lives, these individuals repeatedly find themselves in the same kinds of hurtful relationships that they experienced in childhood. Some settle with mates who constantly berate and belittle them. Others may permit themselves to be repeatedly degraded, attacked, humiliated, or physically injured, and find it difficult to leave these dangerous and violent situations. Sadly, there are those who end up dying at the hands of their abusers every year. Many perpetrators of violence share the same abuse life theme as their victims, but they are overcompensating by taking on the role of the offender. There are also those with this life theme who abuse themselves by ingesting harmful substances or mutilating their bodies. This schema can be summed up as: "I deserve mistreatment."

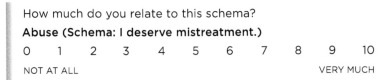

How much do you relate to this schema?
Abuse (Schema: I deserve mistreatment.)

0	1	2	3	4	5	6	7	8	9	10

NOT AT ALL   VERY MUCH

Dependence

The *dependence* theme is characterized by the feeling that one is incapable of surviving on one's own. Individuals who relate to this schema feel inadequate and poorly equipped to handle adult responsibilities. They are like children in adult bodies. They give others the power to dominate them and trust others to know what is best for them rather than trusting in their own judgment. After allowing themselves to be dependent, they often begin to resent their dependency on another. Many find themselves with parents or partners who need them to be dependent. They often come to therapy hoping the therapist will make their decisions for them, as they fear taking responsibility for their own choices. They may allow themselves to be controlled, abused, or deprived in exchange for the security of having someone to take care of them. Often their relationships with their partners favor parent-child dynamics rather than adult-adult interactions. Should a partner exit the relationship, it is not unusual for the person who lives with this theme to become suicidal. One male client who was acting out a dependence theme consistently lost jobs because he expected others to tell him what to do rather than make decisions on his own. His wife was a strong woman who dominated him in the relationship. At one point during our therapy work, he proudly announced, "When I first came to you I felt like I was about thirteen. Now I feel like I am about eighteen, so I am making progress!"

Common among this group are panic attacks and anxiety—particularly agoraphobia, when individuals become fearful of going out in public places and tend to remain at home where they feel safest. Those with the dependence theme may also develop physical illness to solicit caretaking on the part of loved ones and to make it less likely that the other will leave them. Not surprisingly, many people with the dependence spellbound theme also have the abandonment theme operating in their lives. This theme emerges from a childhood in which caregivers were either neglectful or overprotective. This schema can be summed up as: "I do not trust myself."

How much do you relate to this schema?

Dependence (Schema: I do not trust myself.)

0	1	2	3	4	5	6	7	8	9	10
NOT AT ALL										VERY MUCH

Victim

Because of the feeling of powerlessness that typically accompanies trauma, we often decide that we have absolutely no control over what happens to us in life. The person who engages this life theme plays the role of *victim* in his or her life drama. These individuals consistently make choices that have negative consequences, but they feel like helpless victims of life's circumstances. When opportunities for change present themselves, these folks look the other way. People with this theme are rarely proactive and tend to blame other people or circumstances for their unhappiness, and they thrive on self-pity. As a result, they consistently feel powerless to create positive change in their lives. Unlike those with the abuse theme, these individuals are rarely actually being victimized; however, that is how they view themselves and the events that transpire in their lives. One client with the victim theme was deeply unhappy and saw everyone else but herself as responsibility for her unhappy life situation. Due to the bitter resentment she had carried around for decades, she suffered from a multitude of physical disorders. Typically the childhood of the powerless victim was fraught with abuse or neglect. But victimhood can also develop from being pampered and learning to view others as responsible for one's own happiness. This schema can be summed up as: "I am powerless."

How much do you relate to this schema?

Victim (Schema: I am powerless.)

0	1	2	3	4	5	6	7	8	9	10
NOT AT ALL										VERY MUCH

Struggle

When we have had to struggle to survive the ordeals of our early years, it is common for us to hold the perspective that struggle is an integral part of life. Those of us who act out the *struggle* theme make everything harder than it needs to be. We expect it to be difficult to accomplish our goals, and so it is. It does not occur to us to think of ways to make things easier on ourselves because we accept struggle as a way of life. Of course, many accomplishments require dedication and hard work. However, a belief in the necessity of struggle makes us think that if something is worthwhile, achieving it has to hurt, or that we don't deserve to get what we want without pain. It means we may not even recognize that there is an easier path to follow. And even if we see it, we won't choose the joyful path when there is an arduous alternative. This schema can be summed up as: "Life is a painful struggle."

How much do you relate to this schema?

Struggle (Schema: Life is a painful struggle.)

0	1	2	3	4	5	6	7	8	9	10

NOT AT ALL   VERY MUCH

Caretaker

During a traumatic childhood, we may begin to act on the *caretaker* theme, as we come to expect that it is our job to keep everyone else happy. We may have received this message directly from parents who needed us to take care of them and our siblings, or we may have discovered at an early age that the role of caretaker helped us to solicit love and acceptance from others. We become masterful at fostering dependency in others. "As long as they need me, they certainly won't leave me." But in trying to keep everyone else happy (which is of course, an impossible task), we end up sacrificing our own joy and well-being. Individuals who live via the caretaker schema feel guilty and selfish if they do something for themselves or ask for something they need. It is generally very difficult for them to say, "No" to others or to allow others to be responsible for themselves. When everyone else's needs come first, our own needs are ignored; eventually we begin to feel resentful and taken advantage of. Over time, this is a perfect set-up for depression and the development of physical disorders due to lack of self-care. This schema can be summed up as: "I am responsible for everyone else's happiness."

How much do you relate to this schema?

Caretaker (Schema: I am responsible for everyone else's happiness.)

0   1   2   3   4   5   6   7   8   9   10

NOT AT ALL   VERY MUCH

Lack

People who have experienced impoverishment during their early lives often carry that expectation into their adult years, with the theme of *lack*: whatever it is they lacked as children, they expect to lack as adults. For example, if there was not enough money to meet their basic needs when they were children, they do not expect to have enough in adulthood. Thus, if you grew up in poverty, it may be difficult for you to imagine yourself as a prosperous adult. You may find that even when you do have plenty, you experience a looming fear that your abundance is only temporary and will likely be taken away at any moment. People who fear there is not enough tend to be worriers. They worry that even though they have enough money, love, success, joy, or good health today, they may lose it tomorrow. The lack mentality says that there is never enough of what is wanted or needed. Since we always tend to get what we expect—that is, we always make ourselves right—those who decide there isn't enough, tend to experience real deprivation in their lives. They expect to be impoverished, and so they are. Whether they had a lack of financial abundance, love, success, freedom, or joy—their adult lives often continue to be deficient in whatever was missing in their painful childhoods. This schema can be summed up as: "There is not enough."

How much do you relate to this schema?

Lack (Schema: There is not enough.)

0   1   2   3   4   5   6   7   8   9   10

NOT AT ALL   VERY MUCH

Vulnerability

Those with the *vulnerability* spellbound theme are controlled by extreme irrational fears and anxieties that something bad is always about to happen, that they are at risk for illness, financial ruin, accidents, natural disasters, muggings, or terrorist attacks. This theme is common among those whose parents modeled such fears combined with overprotectiveness, those who lived in unsafe conditions in childhood, or those who suffered a major traumatic event in childhood that resulted in serious loss. One client was plagued by worries that something terrible would happen to her or her children. Her worries kept her up at night and she tended to be overprotective with her children just as her parents had been with her. Here we see a spellbound theme being passed from one generation to the next by a well-meaning parent who does not know any better. As she models extreme levels of anxiety and worry about an unsafe world, she prevents her children from venturing forth to explore and experience the fullness of life. She is encouraging them to grow up with the very same negative mental model that plagues her. This schema can be summed up as: "The world is an unsafe place."

How much do you relate to this schema?
Vulnerability (Schema: The world is an unsafe place.)

0	1	2	3	4	5	6	7	8	9	10

NOT AT ALL   VERY MUCH

Defectiveness

Those who operate with the *defectiveness* theme torment themselves for their supposed inadequacies. They see themselves as hopelessly and permanently flawed, and go through their lives with huge inferiority complexes, forever comparing themselves to others and focusing on the ways in which they fall short. These individuals are extremely self-critical, and often overly critical of others. They may avoid taking risks and meeting life's challenges since they are insecure and lack confidence. Some end up as passive victims in relationships with partners who are verbally, emotionally, or physically

NEW SCIENCE NEW BRAIN NEW YOU

abusive. Others repeatedly pursue partners who are uninterested in them, married, or otherwise unavailable. Those with the defectiveness theme may overcompensate by becoming over-achievers, always trying to prove to themselves and to others that they are superior by buying the biggest house, driving the fastest car, rising to the top of their career field, or marrying a powerful, wealthy man or a gorgeous, young woman. Typically, despite their numerous achievements on the outside, they continue to feel defective and inadequate on the inside. While it seems that the defectiveness theme is similar to the undeserving theme, there is a key difference. Those who hold the defectiveness schema overcompensate for certain specific personal inadequacies (whether real or imagined) through their achievements and acquisitions. In contrast, individuals operating under the undeserving life theme generalize that they are bad, and therefore settle for far less than what they desire or are capable of doing or having. The defectiveness theme develops when a person was repeatedly criticized, harshly punished, belittled, rejected, or abused by caregivers, siblings, or peers, in his or her early years. This schema can be summed up as: "I am not good enough."

How much do you relate to this schema?
Defectiveness (Schema: I am not good enough.)

0	1	2	3	4	5	6	7	8	9	10
NOT AT ALL										VERY MUCH

Unrelenting Standards

Those whose spellbound theme is that of *unrelenting standards* must push themselves to be the best, and never feel that they have achieved enough. Constantly under the gun to do more in less time, these people feel tremendous pressure and yet continue to push themselves harder and harder to meet their own impossible perfectionistic expectations. Often they are workaholics who suffer from numerous physical ailments due to the high level of stress caused by this style of living. In childhood, sometimes these individuals were led to believe that they earned love through their achievements—that they were only lovable or of value for what they *did*, not for who they *were*. Others had caregivers who placed unrelenting standards upon themselves, thus setting the example that perfection must be achieved at all costs. It is also possible that the unrelenting standards theme is a way for individuals to compensate for feelings of inferiority, defectiveness, or worthlessness. This schema can be summed up as: "I must be perfect to prove I am of value."

How much do you relate to this schema?
Unrelenting Standards (Schema: I must be perfect to prove I am of value.)

0	1	2	3	4	5	6	7	8	9	10

NOT AT ALL   VERY MUCH

Entitlement

The last common spellbound theme, *entitlement*, is associated with the feeling that one is special and entitled to have whatever he or she wants, even at another's expense. These individuals lack the ability to put themselves in another's shoes. They may become aggressive bullies who terrorize others to get what they want. They may also be impulsive and lack self-discipline. This pattern can result in serious financial difficulties and problems with holding down a job. They may expect others to take care of them, and take advantage of others to the point when others finally say, "No" and refuse to continue offering assistance. These individuals will often send their partners to therapy rather than coming themselves.

I once had a client who brought his wife to couples counseling. They were parents of an infant and a toddler. In addition to caring for the two children, the wife worked twenty hours a week in her husband's business, cleaned their four-thousand-square-foot house weekly, and cooked two meals every night—one for her husband, who insisted upon being served meat, and the other for herself and the toddler, since they were vegetarians. The husband's complaint that brought him to couples counseling? His wife did not have hors d'oeuvres prepared for him when he got home from work.

I learned that the wife initiated divorce proceedings a year later. Sadly, many people with the sense of entitlement do not seek counseling because they do not see themselves as needing to change anything. Everyone else has the problem, not them.

At times, this theme is used as a form of overcompensation for one of the other spellbound themes, like defectiveness or emotional deprivation. In childhood, those with the entitlement theme were usually overindulged and in control of their caregivers. They were not taught to control their impulses and may have had caregivers who also modeled poor impulse control. This schema can be summed up as: "I am special and my needs and wants must always come first."

How much do you relate to this schema?

Entitlement (Schema: I am special and my needs and wants must always come first.)

0	1	2	3	4	5	6	7	8	9	10
NOT AT ALL										VERY MUCH

Be sure to record your highest scores in your journal. You may also want to write down any other spellbound themes and their associated maladaptive schemas that came to mind while you were completing this exercise.

✦

As you have seen, each of these themes points to particular schemas that could be keeping you tethered to the past. When you replace these limiting schemas with others that are more in alignment with your desires, you stimulate the formation of new brain circuitry that, in turn, opens up new pathways of opportunity for you. In chapter 6, you will have the chance to begin to install more desirable schemas to replace maladaptive ones, and break free from the hold that the past has had on you. But first, we take a look at how we can rewire our brains to replace automatic, self-sabotaging thoughts with those that help us feel more confident, peaceful, fulfilled, and engaged in life.

5

Establishing New Patterns of Thought

For survival purposes, our brains are programmed to focus on what is wrong in our world, rather than what is right. In their book, *Buddha's Brain*, Rick Hanson and Richard Mendius point out that the brain is "like Velcro for negative experiences and Teflon for positive ones."[1] This means our brains seek out and remember the negative, while they overlook and forget the positive. When it comes to our everyday lives, it is not difficult to see this principle in action. How easy it is to focus on what is wrong! How often do we notice what is going right in our lives? I am always struck by the way in which a headache can garner my full attention, yet I don't even notice when it has disappeared. While the blister on our right heel keeps pulling at our attention, how much are we noticing how good the left heel feels without any blisters?

When we are spellbound, this tendency to focus on the negative is amplified. We are so accustomed to our typical patterns of thinking that we fail to recognize we are playing the same destructive tapes in our heads, over and over again, that we have been playing for the past twenty or thirty years or more. The messages are so familiar that we don't stop to question their validity or to push the "off" button. We tell ourselves "I'm so inadequate," "No one would ever want to have a relationship with me," or "I can't do anything right." And these thoughts appear to be beyond our control.

Because of their repetitive nature, these automatic thoughts operate as a kind of self-hypnosis. If for years you've told yourself hundreds of times every day that you just can't do math, then guess what? You can't! The best teachers in the world can't overcome that kind of mental programming. One woman who wanted to lose weight but had been unsuccessful for years "caught" herself telling herself how fat she was hundreds of times every day. Finally, she realized that if she was to be successful in losing weight, it was essential that she stop "feeding" herself these negative messages—a form of self-hypnosis that actually worked against her weight-loss efforts.

Spellbound thoughts are rejecting, self-destructive, and self-sabotaging. We tell ourselves we can't do the good things we want to do without dire consequences. "If I take that class, I'll fail; and everyone will know how incompetent I am." "If I try out for that play and get the part, I'll forget my lines and look like a fool." "If I ask that person on a date, I'll be rejected because I am not good enough." "If I quit my job, no one else will hire me because I'm too old."

Through our spellbound lenses, we view people and circumstances in the worst possible light. If there is a possible down side to any situation, we will focus on that. The most joyful events can be turned into a source of pain. The greatest success will be perceived as an utter failure. The most incredible opportunity will be viewed as a set-up for disaster.

Since our worldview is problem-focused, we give primary attention to our own difficulties and to those of others. Life becomes a series of painful predicaments to be dealt with. The more we identify with the trials and tribulations we have endured, the more we use them as the basis for our self-definition. We become afraid of life without our problems, uncertain of who we would be without them. Our thoughts are often catastrophic, jumping to the conclusion that one bump in the road means the end of the road. If one person rejects us, then we tell ourselves that everyone will. If we get one poor grade on a test, then we will never pass the class. If we experience an unfamiliar pain, we are dying. Spellbound thinking seduces us with judgments, generally that we are "better than" or "less than" others. "I'm a loser" or "I'm smarter than that guy" are two sides of the same coin.

Our spellbound thoughts dredge up unhappy events from our history that make us feel guilty, sad, angry, or regretful, and we replay them over and over again. Or, they may fast-forward our minds to a future in which we envision dire consequence coming to pass, evoking feelings of anxiety and fear. All the while, we are distracted from the feeling of well-being that is always available to us in the now.

The best way to know if you are engaging in spellbound thinking is to notice how you feel. Spellbound thinking will always make you feel terrible, whether invoking feelings of depression, anger, frustration, guilt, shame, hopelessness, hurt, or fear. Negative emotions are a helpful signal from your greater Self that you are engaging in harmful habits of thought. Your feelings can be your best guide in identifying the negative thoughts you wish to change, and in monitoring your progress as you shift your thoughts to something more positive and life affirming.

While we often believe that our negative emotions are triggered by the current events in our lives, they are actually a by-product of the things we tell ourselves *about* the events in our lives. For example, when Steve didn't get the job for which he had interviewed, he felt defeated, hopeless, and depressed. These feelings however, were due to the messages he was giving himself, like "No one will ever hire me," and "I didn't get this job because I'm not as good as the other people who applied for it." Although it is natural for Steve to feel some disappointment under the circumstances, he was making himself feel even worse by engaging in catastrophic thinking.

Instead of thinking that this one failed attempt to get hired means he will *never* get hired, Steve could remind himself that this interview was good practice, and that the right job will come along for him if he remains open to it. He might also tell himself that he probably didn't get this job because it wasn't the right or best one for him.

Monitor Your Thinking

Although it may feel as though your thoughts are outside the realm of your control, this is far from the truth. You have ultimate control over your thoughts and, if you desire, you can change patterns of thought that have been familiar to you for a very long time. It may be challenging at first, but if you are determined to think differently, you can and will. Over time, this new way of thinking will become more natural to you as your brain builds neural networks that support your new thought processes. As you practice thinking in ways that trigger uplifting feelings of peace, well-being, joy, optimism, love, and appreciation, those new neural circuits will become increasingly strengthened and dominant. As you stop thinking in the same negative, self-defeating ways, your brain will begin to prune those old neural pathways that are not being used. Over time, it will be easier and easier to engage in the kind of life-affirming thoughts that support you in living a more joyful and satisfying life.

Make an effort to begin noticing your repetitive thought patterns:

- Do you focus more on your positive or your negative attributes?
- Are you more likely to pay attention to what's right or what's wrong in your world?
- Do you tend to dwell on thoughts of appreciation, joy, and delightful anticipation or on problems, misfortune, and doom and gloom?
- Do you speak more about others' assets or their shortcomings?
- Do you recall your most satisfying memories or do you ruminate on past "failures?"
- Are you more likely to see the glass as half empty or half full?
- Do you spend more time thinking about what you want or about what you don't want?

As stated earlier, your emotions give you immediate feedback regarding the kind of thoughts you are entertaining, and whether or not your negative mind is running the show. If you are feeling uplifted, joyful, peaceful, appreciative, passionate, or hopeful, then you are holding positive thoughts, and you are in the process of retraining your brain to focus in a new direction. If however, you are feeling sad, scared, anxious, resentful, regretful, or angry, then your thoughts are most likely on automatic and playing an old recording.

Begin to monitor your feelings throughout the day. Ask yourself "What am I feeling right now? Am I feeling good or bad?" Your answers will enable you to recognize if and when you have reverted back to your automatic spellbound thinking. When you become aware that you are feeling bad, and therefore engaging in spellbound thinking, you need only find a new thought that feels better to you in the moment. For example, if you are thinking about an upcoming test and feeling anxious as you entertain thoughts of failing it, you may choose to tell yourself things like, "I am well-prepared for this exam. I have done well on other similar tests, so I am capable of doing well on this one. I believe I deserve to pass." It is important that whatever you tell yourself makes you feel better. Simply repeating empty words is not helpful, if they do not make a difference in how you are feeling.

If you cannot come up with a thought about the same subject that feels better to you, then you can either focus your mind on a completely different subject that does make you feel good—such as something you appreciate, or something that brings you joy—or you can do something that helps you to feel peaceful, like meditation or guided imagery.

Worry and fear are the result of trying to predict and control the future. They are your attempts at keeping yourself safe in an uncertain world. Although it may feel like you are helping yourself by being anxious about what lies ahead, the truth is that you are actually hurting yourself. Worry and fear are a good sign that you are trying to navigate the river of life by fighting the current. They are prime indicators that you are engaging in spellbound thinking and, thus, working against yourself in the accomplishment of your goals. Worry and fear tend to attract what you don't want, and repel what you do want. And while you are trying so hard to control the future, you are ignoring the one thing you do have total control over: where you focus your attention in the present. This is your point of power.

If you catch yourself feeling worried or fearful about the future, ask yourself, "Is there something I can do about my concerns right now?" If there is, go ahead and do it. If not, let go of the worry and fear and imagine that things will turn out just the way you want. For example, if you are worried about growing older and weaker, imagine instead feeling stronger and more capable as you age. If you fear getting sick, picture your immune system functioning at optimal levels. Should you dread giving a speech, imagine thundering applause following your splendid performance.

Still another way to awaken from your negative trance is to shift your attention from things you don't want to things you do want. Remember, our critical minds encourage us to pay the most attention to those things in our lives that are wrong, bad, or missing rather than those things that are right, good, and present. We are seduced into focusing more on our liabilities than on our assets. We complain about what *isn't* working in our lives, and remain oblivious to what *is* working. We zero in on our partner's faults and ignore their best attributes. We put our deficiencies under a microscope while remaining blind to our greatest gifts.

Whatever we focus on in our lives increases. The more we focus on what we don't want, the worse it gets. Conversely, the more we focus on what we do want, the better it gets. Another way of saying this is that *whatever we focus on becomes our reality.* This means that just by beginning to give your attention to what's right in your life, you can begin to transform it in positive ways. The following exercise will help you refocus your attention on what is right in your life.

EXERCISE 5 FOCUSING ON THE GOOD IN YOUR LIFE

1. Choose a day and see how many good things you can notice and acknowledge to yourself during that day. Try to notice things you normally take for granted or ignore. Pretend you are experiencing everything for the first time. Notice everything and everyone that is a positive force in your life. Notice

your own good qualities. Notice the things that go well that day. Pay attention to little things, like the way the clouds look in the sky, the smile of a friend, the feeling of warm water washing over you in the shower, the smell of coffee brewing, or the sound of a favorite song on the radio. Become consciously aware of the feelings of well-being these things create.

2. Get in touch with a feeling of gratitude for all the blessings in your life. While alone at home or while driving by yourself in the car, recite out loud "I am grateful for . . ." and see how many times you can complete that sentence.

3. At the end of the day, take time to record your observations in your journal.

What Did You Experience?
* What was this experience like for you?
* Did anything about this experience surprise you?
* What would you like most to remember about this experience?
* How might you put what you learned into action on a daily basis?

✦

Monitor Your Words

Since whatever we focus on becomes our reality, it is also helpful to watch what you choose to talk about. Do you find yourself recounting tales of hardship and woe on a frequent basis? Are you often likely to be discussing your own misfortunes and/or the misfortunes of others? Do you spend long hours discussing what's wrong with the world?

This, too, can become a troublesome habit, and one that keeps you attracting more of the same into your life. It is not just what we focus on that becomes our reality—it is also what we talk about. Talk about problems, and you are actually unwittingly perpetuating them. It is as if you were pouring cement on those very situations that you most want to have *out* of your life—solidifying them and making them stay put. Remember, whatever we focus on tends to get bigger in our lives. Talk about what is working in your life, and you are likely to experience more of that. (Of course, the exception is when you choose to speak to a counselor with the intention of finding solutions for your current difficulties. This is not the same as simply complaining about your problems. Rather, it is taking action to resolve them.)

It's always easy to find something negative to focus our discussions on, and this habit tends to keep us feeling depressed, powerless, and hopeless. I am not suggesting that you stick your head in the sand or deny that serious problems exist in your own life or in the lives of others. Nor am I saying that you have to pretend that things are wonderful when they are terrible. Rather, I am saying that spending countless hours recounting how bad things are is not helpful to you or to anyone else. Shift the focus of your conversations with self and others to the positive, and know that you are planting the seeds of transformation in your life!

6

Installing
New Schemas

No matter what spellbound themes we may be acting out, we always have the power in the present to break the spell of the past and awaken to a more joyful and satisfying life. One way of doing this is to install new mental models that are more in alignment with the life we want to be living. By installing new schemas in our consciousness, we shift our default mode, thereby creating changes in our world from the inside out. Revising our schemas requires that we make use of our intuitive, emotional, symbolic right-brain mode of processing, as explained in chapters 1 and 2. This enables us to access the nonverbal parts of our brain where our implicit memories and the mental models that are derived from them are encoded. Our goal is to install new mental models and to repeatedly activate the synaptic pathways associated with these alternate and more life-affirming ways of viewing ourselves, others, and the world we live in. Using the thirteen spellbound themes from chapter 4, what follows is a guide for how to start installing new mental models.

Identify the New Schemas You Want to Install

Begin by identifying one spellbound theme that's currently prevalent in your life and that you would like to change. Write down the maladaptive schema associated with this theme, and then write down the positive schemas you would like to install in its place. You may include positive schemas from the following list or you may create your own. These new schemas (also called affirmations) should be stated in positive terms, they should be brief, and they should make you feel good when you say them out loud. Here are some suggestions for positive schemas that are possible replacements for each of the negative ones identified in chapter 4.

ABANDONMENT
Schema: People I love always abandon me.
New Schemas
* I am enough.
* I choose to include loving people in my life who are loyal and true.
* My partner and I easily allow one another the space to develop, grow, and thrive.
* I surround myself with people who are always there for me, as I am for them.

MISTRUST
Schema: Other people cannot be trusted.
New Schemas
* I attract people who treat me with respect and loving-kindness.
* I surround myself with people who are trustworthy.
* I choose friends and lovers who are worthy of my trust.
* I let love in.
* I easily notice the beauty in others.

UNDESERVING
Schema: I am unworthy.
New Schemas
* I am worthy.
* I deserve the best that life has to offer.
* I deserve (love, relaxation, financial abundance, success, joy, good health, etc.).

- I allow my highest good to come to me easily.
- I am worthy of having and enjoying what I desire.

ABUSE
Schema: I deserve mistreatment.
New Schemas
- I surround myself with people who treat me with kindness and respect.
- I deserve to be treated with kindness and respect.
- I am worthy of love.
- All my relationships are mutually kind and respectful.
- I allow myself to be loved.
- I treat myself in loving ways.

DEPENDENCE
Schema: I do not trust myself.
New Schemas
- It is easy for me to trust and follow my inner guidance.
- I trust myself to know what is best for me.
- I joyfully and courageously follow my dreams.
- I take responsibility for my physical, mental, emotional, and spiritual well-being.
- I now find the courage, strength, and confidence to act in accordance with my inner wisdom.

VICTIM
Schema: I am powerless.
New Schemas
- I now create my life just as I want it.
- I exercise my personal power by making healthy choices.
- I embrace my power to make a positive difference.
- I am capable of doing anything I set my mind to doing.
- I now awaken to my beauty, power, and greatest potential.

STRUGGLE
Schema: Life is a painful struggle.
New Schemas
- Good things come easily to me now.
- I attract my highest good easily and joyfully.
- I deserve a life of ease and joy.
- I release the need to struggle.
- I surrender to my highest good now.

CARETAKER
Schema: I am responsible for everyone else's happiness.
New Schemas
- I now honor and voice my own needs and wants.
- I give myself permission to say "no" to others.
- I allow others to be responsible for their own happiness.
- I take good care of myself.

LACK
Schema: There is not enough.
New Schemas
- I am grateful for the abundance that flows into my life easily.
- I now have all the (time, money, love, success, joy, friendships, creativity, etc.) I desire.
- I am now open to receive an unlimited supply of (money, love, success, joy, friendships, creativity, etc.).

VULNERABILITY
Schema: The world is an unsafe place.
New Schemas
- I focus on enjoying the present moment.
- I trust myself to deal with whatever life brings.
- In this moment, I am safe and all is well.
- I place my attention on all the good in my life and in the world around me.

DEFECTIVENESS
Schema: I am not good enough.

New Schemas

* I am good enough.
* I accept and appreciate myself as I am.
* It is easy for me to focus on and acknowledge my strengths.
* I celebrate my uniqueness.

UNRELENTING STANDARDS
Schema: I must be perfect to prove I am of value.

New Schemas

* I am perfectly imperfect.
* I know my value comes from who I am rather than from what I do.
* I allow myself the freedom to make mistakes and learn from them.
* I take the time to enjoy each moment and savor its goodness.
* I allow myself to relax, play, and enjoy life.

ENTITLEMENT
Schema: I am special and my needs
and wants must always come first.

New Schemas

* I humble myself easily and own my weaknesses, foibles, and limitations.
* I put myself in others' shoes to understand what they think and feel.
* I recognize that others' needs matter, and I strive to have equal give and take in my relationships.
* I treat others with honor and respect.

◆

Pay close attention to how you feel as you say or write a particular schema or affirmation. You should feel uplifted, hopeful, or encouraged as you repeat it. If you feel worse instead of better, or if you feel nothing at all as you say it, find another affirmation that has a more positive effect on you.

For example, Emma wanted to change the schema that she would never find someone to love her. She began to tell herself "I have a wonderful life partner," but found that those words just made her feel worse about being alone. However, when she told herself, "I have many friends who love me," "I have a lot to offer in a relationship," and "I deserve to have a loving partner," she felt uplifted and optimistic about her future. This was a signal that these affirmations were the right ones for her to be using at the time.

Establish the Intention to Install the New Schema

Once you have identified one or more affirmations that feel good, the next step is to be very clear with yourself that you intend to release the old way of thinking and to replace it with the new attitude. There is tremendous power in establishing a clear intention. Your intention represents a strong desire that you are using to fuel the engine of change. It is a signal for all your internal resources to align and assist you in the accomplishment of your objective.

Speak Your Affirmations and Write Them Down

Begin to state the new schema to yourself many times daily; write it down, giving it your full attention as you do so. Make it your personal mantra. Any time you catch yourself thinking in the old way, replace those thoughts with your new affirmation. Here you are using repetition as a form of self-hypnosis, so the more you repeat your schema, the better—as long as it feels uplifting to say it. This repetition is also important to your brain as it provides mental rehearsal and establishes the new neural pathways corresponding to your new mental model.

Look for Evidence in Your Life
That Your New Schema Is True

Consciously and deliberately keep an eye out for circumstances that validate your new mental model. Look for signs that your new way of thinking is in alignment with reality. For example, if you are affirming that you are surrounded by people you can trust and who treat you with respect and kindness, take note of each person whom you encounter on your path who fills this description.

Be sure to recall experiences from your past that are also in alignment with your new schema. Our tendency is to forget about life events that do not fit our current view of reality. It is likely that you have already had certain experiences in the distant or recent past that can be used to reinforce your new way of seeing things. For example, if you are affirming that you trust and follow your inner guidance, remember times in the past when you trusted your own judgment and things turned out even better than you had hoped.

Activate the Power of Pretend

Employ the power of your right brain's processing mode by pretending that you already hold your new mental model as your predominant view of reality. For example, if you want to believe that you can trust yourself, act as if you already do. Throughout the day, ask yourself, "How would I behave in this situation if I trusted myself?" As you try out new ways of behaving, see yourself as practicing to play a new role in your own life.

Sometimes it helps to think of another person—either someone you know or someone you know of—who appears to have the qualities, lifestyle, and attitude you desire. As you go about your day, pretend to be that person. When you are faced with challenging situations, ask yourself how that person would view the situation, and how he or she would most likely handle it. By pretending to be someone else and trying out a new repertoire of behaviors, you can discover strengths you didn't know you had.

Play with Your Imagination

You can use your imagination to become more familiar with how it feels to hold your new mental model. The more comfortable you are envisioning your new life, the more quickly it will become a part of your reality. Use the following exercise as a springboard for playing with your imagination.

EXERCISE 6   INSTALLING A NEW SCHEMA

1. Choose one new schema you would like to install during this exercise.

2. Sit or lie down in a comfortable position. Make sure your spine is straight and your legs are uncrossed. Close your eyes and begin taking long, slow, deep breaths. Allow yourself plenty of time for every breath. Notice the rising and falling of the area below your navel as you inhale and exhale. Imagine that you are inhaling peace, up through the soles of your feet. Every time you exhale, feel yourself letting go of all tension, just letting it drain away. Take all the time you need to feel more and more calm and comfortable. You might imagine that you are surrounded by a beautiful cocoon of light. You might picture it as golden light or another color or colors, or just sense its presence around you. Experience the cocoon embracing you with safety, serenity, and love. Allow the light of that cocoon to be absorbed into each cell, spreading peace and relaxation, as if all your cells were producing a beautiful note in perfect harmony. Note that each cell absorbs just the amount it needs to be replenished and restored. Experience your body responding at it becomes more and more relaxed, surrendering to the serenity and comfort of this moment. Notice your mind becoming as calm and clear as a deep blue sky on a cloudless summer day as it, too, is saturated with peace. Give yourself permission to take this minivacation as you prepare to venture even more deeply within, if you desire.

3. Now imagine that the area around your heart is easily opening up and expanding until you again become aware of a special doorway. The doorway leads directly into your heart sanctuary—a place that is completely safe, peaceful, nurturing, and loving. It may resemble a favorite place you visited in the past, or someplace you have just created. Fill in all the details exactly to your liking. Engage as many of your senses as you can. In this setting, you can access your unlimited potential for creativity, inner guidance, self-transformation, and self-healing. Everything about your heart sanctuary is exactly as you want it to be. Use all your senses now to imagine exactly how it looks, smells, feels, tastes, and sounds here in your heart sanctuary. Feel every level of your being becoming filled with the serenity and love that are so abundantly available here. Drink it in and allow it to nurture every cell of your being. Notice how safe you feel, how completely supported, how calm and peaceful.

4. In your heart sanctuary, you find the perfect spot in which to sit or lie down and bring to mind one of the new, positive schemas you want to install in the core of your being. Allow an image, symbol, or picture to come to mind that represents this new schema. It is important to allow this to develop. Simply be still and open, and create the space for it to present itself to you. Once the image, symbol, or picture that represents this new schema comes into your consciousness, notice everything you can about it and your reaction to it. Just accept it as a gift from your deeper Self and know that the meaning will reveal itself in time. You may notice that it is pulsating with beautiful, radiant light. You may see this image, symbol, or picture clearly, or just get a general sense of it. However you imagine it is perfect.

5. If you choose, imagine you are putting that image, symbol, or picture into the center of your heart and that the light it emits

is spreading throughout your body. As you do so, imagine that the new schema is becoming an integral part of you. Observe as its positive message is transported throughout your body through your veins and arteries. Notice what this experience feels like as you simply allow the process to take place.

6. Imagine that a tiny version of the symbol, picture, or image is being implanted in the DNA of every cell of your body. Sense your cells welcoming this new, positive message. Imagine the new schema is becoming more and more a natural part of your being—as natural as the beating of your heart.

7. Spend some time imagining what kind of life is possible for you as you begin to accept and act upon this new schema as your new reality. Play with your imagination. Let it soar. Imagine you are stepping into a brand new reality, in which your new, positive schema is reflected all about you. Pretend your life is like a movie, the most wonderful, satisfying, joyful, fulfilling movie you have ever seen. Make it as real as you can. Fill it in with lots of details. Get excited about what you are experiencing. Be playful. Think big. What is your life like? What does it feel like to live in this brand new reality? What are you able to do now, that you weren't able to do before? What new opportunities does it open up for you? What changes are suddenly possible that were not possible until now? How does it alter your way of being in the world? Imagine how it feels to be going through your day with this new schema pulsating through your being. What changes do you envision in how you think, feel, and behave? Feel yourself adjusting to this new reality, becoming comfortable with it, until it feels very natural to you.

8. Ask yourself what little steps you can take every day to practice acting in accordance with your new schema. This might involve treating yourself more kindly, talking to yourself in a different way, taking a little step out of your comfort zone

to initiate a conversation with someone you don't know well, doing a good deed for someone else, asking for what you need, saying "no," or changing a critical thought about another person to a more compassionate or understanding thought.

9. Slowly, begin to prepare yourself to awaken and return to the room. Thank the images for coming and begin to feel your body by wiggling your fingers and toes. When you are ready to awaken completely, tell yourself that you are coming back, feeling clearheaded, refreshed, and alert. Open your eyes, stretch, and feel yourself returning fully and completely to the present moment.

10. Take some time to record your experience in your journal. Record at least ten little things you could do to practice acting in accordance with your new schema. Establish the intention of doing at least one of those things every day. At the end of each day, write down what you did.

What Did You Experience?
* Were there any surprises?
* How did it feel to install the new schema?
* What would you most like to remember about this experience?

◆

As you do this exercise, you are forming new neural circuits in your brain that are in accordance with a new way of being. Remember that repetition is important in creating new neural networks. Use this guided imagery often and practice your new behaviors every day. Your brain will continue to strengthen these new healing pathways each time you do so!

The following exercise is another way of reinforcing your new ways of thinking, feeling, and behaving in accordance with your new mental model. It also taps into the right brain's processing mode, and is therefore a powerful way of continuing to implant seeds of change in your consciousness.

EXERCISE 7   LETTER FROM A FUTURE SELF

1. Based upon your experience in exercise 6, pretend three years have passed, and your life is now a perfect reflection of the new schema you have installed. Write a letter to a dear friend who has not heard from you over the past three years. Tell your friend all about the new life you are now living. Allow yourself to think big here! Write about how it feels to be experiencing the fulfillment of your dreams. Write about how you spend your days, what thrills and excites you, your successes and accomplishments, your relationships, your career, and your personal development. Write about what you do for fun, your creative endeavors, and what brings you your greatest pleasure.

2. Read your letter often and continue to add to it as new ideas occur to you.

Practice the preceding exercises often, for each time you do, the new neural pathways you are creating are strengthened. As this happens, you will find it becomes easier and more natural for you to think in new, more expansive, and creative ways about yourself and your life. This is a sign that you are beginning to awaken from your spellbound state.

7

Cultivating Awareness

When we are under the spell of our past, it is as if we were asleep. We operate unconsciously, as if in a trance. We are on automatic pilot, thinking the same thoughts for decades. Fueled by our volatile emotions, we engage in knee-jerk reactions to people and situations. We feel somehow incomplete and unsettled within and may have the sense that we are waiting for our "real" lives to begin. We are subject to the whims of our minds and our emotions as they carry us off in whatever direction they choose to go from moment to moment. We are tormented by uncomfortable thoughts and feelings about the past, or anxiety and worries about the future, that keep us from being fully present in the now. We get caught up in the drama of our everyday lives and lose sight of the big picture.

If you recognize yourself in this description, welcome to the human race! You are not alone. Most of us can relate to this way of being to a greater or lesser extent. Your spellbound patterns are, in great part, driven by factors that have not been under your conscious control. While you have been along for the ride, it may feel like someone else has been driving the car. It is important to refrain from judging yourself for what you have or have not done in the past. A much better place to focus your energy and attention is on doing those things now that will help you gain control of the vehicle and steer it in the direction you want to go. This is best accomplished through cultivating present-moment awareness.

To be aware is to be fully conscious and intentional in what you do. When you are aware, you're *observing* your mind and emotions rather than ignoring them, judging them, or getting swept away by them. When you are aware, you are fully present in your life. Your responses to challenging situations are conscious and deliberate rather than unconscious and reactive.

Each time you cultivate your capacity for awareness, you activate and develop the higher region of your brain—the orbitofrontal cortex and the anterior cingulate—that serves an integrative function.[1] As discussed in earlier chapters, when we become spellbound, our memories of traumatic events and our reactions to them are locked in our limbic system and stored as nonverbal implicit memories. This means we do not have access to our higher brain regions when these memories are triggered by present life events that in some way resemble the original traumatic episodes. During those moments, we are flooded with emotion and the urge to take action to deal with what our limbic system perceives as danger, without the benefit of our reasoned, logical cortex. We act to relieve our internal distress, but these spellbound reactions only make things worse, not better.

Developing your ability to be mindful in the present moment is your escape hatch from these automatic reactions. By expanding and strengthening the neural pathways of your prefrontal cortex, you will be able to engage your higher brain centers when you need them most. These higher brain centers are capable of assessing the current situation for the degree of danger, modulating your emotions, and thinking through and initiating the best course of action. During stressful life events, rather than acting on automatic pilot by losing your temper, reaching for the next candy bar, lashing out in anger, collapsing with feelings of inadequacy, or freezing up and going mute, you will discover a newfound capacity to be fully aware and present, able to think clearly, and capable of determining the optimal response in the moment. The more you practice entering a state of present-moment awareness, the more you will build and strengthen the neural circuits that will enable you to retire your spellbound reactions in favor of responding in a wise, reasoned, and calm manner to whatever challenges life may bring along your journey. In this way, you are able to tap into the remarkable capabilities of the thinking mind while avoiding its pitfalls.

There are numerous other rewards that also come with practice in being mindful. This state of being opens us up to a realm of limitless possibilities and vast creative potential. We are able to access profound states of peace and well-being, tap into our intuitive knowing, experience greater wisdom and mental acuity, connect with our inner guidance for answers and solutions, and view our lives from a big-picture perspective. This expanded state of consciousness—called *awakened presence*—enables us to feel deep love and compassion and uncover previously hidden qualities like courage, confidence, and resiliency.

Mindfulness brings fluidity to our lives—an openness to experience as it unfolds from moment to moment—rather than rigidity. There is a sense of great aliveness and attunement to other beings and the earth itself. Your cells thrive in the light of presence, making it an optimal state for maintaining physical health and well-being, and for slowing down the body's aging process.[2]

Doorways for Entering the State of Presence

This state of heightened realization exists within you, just beyond the incessant chatter of your mind. By entering a state of presence, you can discover a quality of aliveness, joy, and peace that surpasses words. Each moment that you spend experiencing the vast, limitless sea of pure consciousness that is you on the inner plane, it becomes easier to find your way there the next time. Of course, I refer to this state as if it had a location when it is actually no-place and everywhere you are. But for the sake of grasping the concept, it can be helpful to think of the state of presence as if it had a location, a place that we visit that lies beyond the mind. Although this may sound mystical and out of reach for all but the yogis of India or Buddhist monks, entering a state of alive presence is actually highly accessible to each of us. We need only to know where to find the doorway into that experience, and then practice entering it.

How do you know when you are "there"—that you are experiencing the kind of presence I am describing? First, you will feel completely peaceful—yet fully alive and aware. You may experience a sense of expansiveness. There will be moments, brief at first, of no-thought at all when you may note the difference between knowing and thinking. When thoughts do occur, you will find yourself able to witness them without judgment and with the recognition that you are not your thoughts. In this way, you will be able to observe them without being swept away by them.

So—how do you find and enter this place? Let's take a look at some of the doorways you can use to access the experience of heightened awareness.

BRING YOUR ATTENTION FULLY TO THE PRESENT MOMENT

One thing all the passageways to greater awareness have in common is that they all exist in the present moment. Typically, our minds keep us occupied by taking us back to the past or forward to the future, generating fear and uneasiness and filling our heads with incessant chattering. When we are in our heads, we are not in a state of awareness—rather, we are preoccupied with the mind's gymnastics. By bringing our attention fully into the now, we access a variety of doorways into the deeper aspect of Self. There is actually little for our minds to do when we are fully engaged in the present moment. At these times, our minds are more likely to be quiet, and during the brief gaps in our mind's nonstop chatter, we are can momentarily experience the peaceful and expansive state of presence. We may then discover that when our mind is quiet, we can enter a realm of pure awareness. Though this experience may be very brief at first, the positive effects from these moments are cumulative. The following exercise is a means of bringing your attention fully into the present moment.

EXERCISE 8 CULTIVATING PRESENT-MOMENT AWARENESS

You will need to spend at least twenty minutes in a natural setting for this exercise, as you will be taking a walk. You don't need to have a destination in mind. You can visit a favorite nature trail, a neighborhood park, or a small garden.

1. Begin the exercise by walking slowly. Your goal is to remain aware of what you experience through all your senses during the entire time, without analysis or judgment. This means you do not label or critique what you are or are not perceiving, nor treat yourself unkindly as you engage in this process. In order to keep yourself focused on what you perceive in the moment, from time to time, mentally complete each of the following sentences:

   "Right now, I am seeing _____."
   "Right now, I am hearing _____."
   "Right now, I am feeling _____."
   "Right now, I am smelling _____."
   "Right now, I am tasting _____."

2. Attempt to notice everything you can about your surroundings. Pretend that you are seeing, hearing, feeling, tasting, and smelling things for the first time, and try to notice new things about these sensations. Without engaging your thinking, allow yourself to bask in the beauty of nature. Behold the color, form, and scent of a flower, the loveliness of a tree, or the exquisite sound of a gently flowing stream. Let these experiences penetrate to the center of your being.

3. Next, sit down for a few minutes and close your eyes in order to focus more on what you hear, feel, taste, and smell.

4. Should you find that your mind has wandered away from the present, simply bring your awareness back to what you

perceive in the moment, without judging or berating yourself. It is natural for your mind to wander.

5. Afterward, record in your journal some of your experiences and observations.

What Did You Experience?
- Were there any surprises?
- How did it feel to do this exercise?
- What would you most like to remember from this experience?

✦

Make it your daily intent to catch yourself when you have left the now and bring yourself back to it. A good way to know when your attention has wandered from the present moment is to notice how you are feeling. Generally, if you are feeling bad—worried, anxious, guilty, resentful, or fearful—your mind has again led you astray by following a maladaptive pathway. Once you recognize this, it is only a matter of returning to the only time there is—the present moment—without berating or judging yourself. Each time you go through this process, you make it easier to remain present-focused and take one more step toward awakening from your spellbound state.

There are many other activities that can help us to anchor our attention in the now. Some of these include: hiking in a natural setting, planting a garden, interacting with animals, or listening to beautiful music. Physical activity can also be very effective in keeping our attention in the present and giving us a wonderful "brain break." This may include activities like jogging, swimming, dancing, biking, rollerblading, or just walking. You may be attracted to the inner glow you experience in the aftermath of a yoga, Pilates, or Tai Chi session. Or perhaps you enjoy becoming one with the process of creating, whether you are writing, painting, crocheting, sculpting, quilting, building, beading, carving, or cooking. Whatever you choose, practice giving it your full attention in the now and observe how time stands still, your mind becomes quiet, and you begin to experience the peace and well-being that surpasses description.

TURN YOUR ATTENTION INWARD

Most methods for cultivating awareness involve turning our attention within. In today's fast-paced world, we are usually encouraged to be outer focused: unless we are "doing something productive," many of us are afraid we are wasting time. Too often, we compare ourselves to others and determine our personal value on the basis of our accomplishments. We weigh and measure our self-worth based on how many books we have read, degrees we have earned, hours we have exercised, opponents we have beaten, pounds we have lost, titles we have attained, or dollars we have accumulated. Compared to these more seductive pursuits, it appears at first that there is little reward for being still and going within. If anything, we feel guilty taking time to feel peaceful in the present when so many things remain on our to-do list. What's more, when we're spellbound, we would rather do anything rather than look inside ourselves because we fear what we will find lurking there. If only we can keep ourselves busy enough, there is no danger that we will have a moment free to focus within. Yet, until we choose to stop everything and turn inside, we will never know true peace and fulfillment. In avoiding our inner landscape, we prevent ourselves from accessing our great strength and vast creative potential. What's more, the absence of our attention on our inner realm keeps us from experiencing vital aliveness and well-being.

BECOME THE WITNESS TO YOUR
THOUGHTS AND EMOTIONS

Mindfulness meditation is like a form of strength training for your brain as you learn to witness your thoughts and emotions, without allowing them to carry you away from the present moment. As you bring your mind gently and repeatedly back to a point of focus, and become the observer of your mind, you enter a passageway that leads to the state of awakened presence. Many believe that meditation is difficult and that years of special instruction are required to meditate properly. Nothing could be further from the truth. Meditation is the most natural experience in the world. It is you connecting with your inner Self, in the quiet and calm of your being. It is as simple as closing your eyes and focusing on your breathing, as you will see in the following exercise.

EXERCISE 9   AWARENESS MEDITATION

1. Find a place to sit or lie down where you will be undisturbed for whatever period of time you intend to meditate. Often it is better to sit when meditating so that you do not fall asleep. It is fine to begin with periods as brief as five minutes and gradually build up to twenty or thirty minutes or more, depending upon what works for you.

2. Begin by taking a few deep, relaxing breaths, focusing on the gentle rising and falling of your abdomen. Allow your breath to breathe itself, without forcing or controlling it. Notice how it feels to be inhaling and exhaling completely. Attempt to track each breath from start to finish. You may wish to count each breath, from one to five or from one to ten, and then beginning at one again. As you do this, your mind will inevitably wander. When you notice this has happened, gently redirect your attention back to your breath, without judging yourself or becoming frustrated. Know that your wandering mind is to be expected—it is a part of the process, and there is nothing wrong when this happens.

3. After a short while, you may wish to experience yourself surrendering to the experience of your breath and allowing yourself to be completely at one with the process.

4. While continuing to use your breath as a point of focus, allow yourself to *witness* the thoughts, sensations, and emotions

that set up and then disappear against the backdrop of greater conscious awareness. Avoid labeling them as good or bad, or right or wrong, and refrain from trying to change them in any way. Rather, hold an accepting attitude toward them, without getting tangled with them. Watch them as you would clouds passing overhead against a clear blue sky. There is nothing to do but observe them as they come and go, come and go. Picture yourself as that clear, vast blue sky with the clouds of thought and emotion, sensation, and perception, just passing through.

5. During this experience, you may notice an increasing sense of expansiveness, peace, and openness. If this does not happen, refrain from judging yourself as doing something wrong. Whatever you experience, it is perfect in the now. The fact that you are practicing present awareness is what matters, for each moment you spend in this meditation, you are building new neural circuits that will serve you in countless ways.

6. Return to the room slowly whenever you would like. Observe how you feel and spend a few moments recording your experiences in your journal.

◆

There are infinite variations to the preceding meditation. You may choose anything you would like to focus on. Rather than your breath, it may be the flame of a candle, the song of a bird, the sound of a fountain, a favorite static image, or a word or phrase which is silently repeated and synchronized with your breathing, such as "I am love," "Peace," or a favorite line from a prayer. Choose whatever works best for you. What is most important, is that you take time, however brief, to engage in this practice on a regular basis.

In recent years, much research has been done to track the impact of meditation on the brain. Results indicate that an eight-week training program in meditation with healthy subjects provided a demonstrable change in their brains with an associated strengthening of their immune systems.[3] In addition, a 2009 study found evidence that long-term meditators have increased grey matter in the two parts of the brain known to play a key integrative role—the hippocampus and the orbitofrontal cortex. These regions are known to be active when we appraise and regulate our negative emotions and when we demonstrate flexibility in our manner of responding to challenging situations—behaviors which have been found to be typical of meditators in other studies.[4]

TAKE YOUR ATTENTION INTO YOUR PHYSICAL BODY

In his profound book *The Power of Now,* Eckhart Tolle suggests focusing on our invisible, inner body as a form of meditation.[5] This is a wonderful way of transcending the mind and experiencing the state of presence. When we place our attention in our bodies, there is an immediate quieting of the mind, and with it, the possibility of opening to greater awareness.

EXERCISE 10   ENTERING THE BODY

1. To enter into the silent space within, sit in a quiet space, close your eyes, and focus on the life force in your hands, your feet, your arms, and your legs—that part of your body that is below your neck. Try not to picture it, but just to experience it—to sense its aliveness.

2. Next, feel the invisible network of energy that breathes movement and sensation into every cell. Sense the entire pattern of energy that forms your invisible inner body as a complete, dynamic whole. Try not to get too attached to what it might look like. Just feel it. This experience of mindful attention may enable you to experience the expansiveness and aliveness of your inner being.

3. When you are ready, come back slowly to the room. Wiggle your fingers and toes and begin to feel yourself returning to this time and place. Be sure to record your experiences in your journal, noting how this exercise felt, what you want most to remember from this experience, and anything that surprised you.

◆

FOCUS ON SPACE AND STILLNESS

Still another doorway to the state of presence is to focus on space and stillness. When we place our attention on the spaces between our breaths, the space between notes in a beautiful piece of music, the space in the sky beyond the clouds, the space between words being spoken, the spaces between our thoughts, or the spaces between the leaves and branches of tree, it can help to transport us to a different dimension of experience—one in which our mind is at rest. You will find that, within these spaces, there is the quality of perfect stillness. Try the following guided imagery to experience the expansive spaces within your body.

EXERCISE 11   THE UNIVERSE WITHIN

1. Find a comfortable place to sit or lie down. Make sure it is quiet and that you will not be interrupted for fifteen to twenty minutes.

2. Imagine that a beautiful beam of light is coming down from the heavens, directly into the top of your head. Feel this uplifting, radiant light filling your entire being. With each deep and relaxing breath, experience this light penetrating to the very depths of your being. Take all the time you want to bask in the peace and love of this light.

3. Begin to place your attention on the billions of atoms that comprise your physical body. Notice that these atoms are like planets and stars. Observe that within each atom there are vast, silent, spaces comprised of pure stillness. Go into these spaces with your consciousness and observe how it feels to experience them.

4. Notice now, the vast, silent, limitless spaces between the atoms that are also filling with this light. These spaces are proportionately as vast as the spaces between stars in the heavens. Take your awareness into these spaces, and note the deep, profound stillness you find there. Focus on the unlimited universe that exists within you.

5. If your mind begins to wander, or chatter about this and that, just observe without judgment and gently take your attention back into the universe within you. Go again into the silent, vast, spaces between the atoms, and just allow yourself to be. There is nothing to do, accomplish, or learn. At some point, you will find yourself feeling very peaceful and in a state of mindful awareness. Again, just notice.

6. When you are ready to return, do so slowly and gradually. Open your eyes, and come back to this time and place. Congratulate yourself on having taken the time to engage in this process, no matter what the experience was like for you. The practice itself is what matters most—not the outcome.

7. Take time to write in you journal about this practice.

What Did You Experience?
- What was this like for you?
- What, if anything, surprised you during this meditation?
- What would you like to remember about this experience?

✦

REPLACE RESISTANCE WITH ACCEPTANCE

When you accept what life brings to you in each moment, you align with your greater Self and open yourself to the state of presence. Acceptance doesn't mean you are passive when faced with an unpleasant circumstance. It is not an attitude of resignation or the willingness to allow others to mistreat you. Rather, it means you don't waste emotional energy feeling sorry for yourself, you don't blame yourself or others, or resent the situation in which you find yourself. Acceptance is making peace with your present conditions—no matter how difficult they may be, or unfair they seem. Acceptance is holding the premise that everything ultimately happens for your highest good, as you view the big picture of your life through the eyes of your inner Self. Acceptance takes you to a place of inner strength and calm, from which you can best identify and then follow the most effective course of action.

The opposite of acceptance is resistance. When we resist a situation, we engage our minds in judging or interpreting the situation as wrong, bad, terrible, or a mistake. We push against whatever is happening. We say to ourselves such things as, "This should not be happening to me," "This isn't fair," "This isn't right," "This person should behave differently." Resistance is a push against a negative or undesired situation. It is our mind criticizing, reacting against, resenting, or finding fault with a person or situation. Whatever we resist, persists. In other words, the more we resist a situation, the more it stays the same.

For example, you are driving on your way to an important business meeting when you suddenly have a tire blow out. As you steer the car safely to the side of the road, you begin to curse under your breath: "Why me? This had to happen today! I'll probably lose the best business opportunity of my life because of this!" You become furious, frustrated, and completely beside yourself. Perhaps you blame your spouse for not wanting to replace the tires last month. Perhaps you blame your mechanic for not noticing that your tires needed replacing. Perhaps you blame the road construction crew for failing to clear debris from the road.

All this is your mind having a field day with this event—engaged in judging, criticizing, catastrophizing, blaming, and pushing against what is: the fact that you have a flat tire. None of this helps you get the tire repaired.

What if you approached this same situation from a place of acceptance? This would mean that you do not engage your mind in its game of faultfinding, overreacting, and working yourself into a place of heightened upset. Rather, you accept that you have a flat tire. You acknowledge that it is unfortunate, it is certainly not what you would want or choose, but it is what you must deal with. Rather than wasting mental energy pushing against the fact of the flat tire, you would be calm, reasoned, and able to think clearly to solve the problem—engaging your higher brain centers rather than reacting from the emotional signals coming from the limbic system. You stay in the present and do what you must do to have the tire repaired. You do not allow your mind to engage in worries about the consequences of this event. Perhaps you call someone who will also be attending the meeting to explain that you have been delayed. You assume that you will deal with the fallout of this event when the time comes.

It can be difficult to lasso in the mind when it has been accustomed to resisting life's most challenging episodes. What's more, some circumstances are so painful and overwhelming, that it is almost impossible for most of us to move quickly to a place of acceptance. Losing a loved one, facing the destruction of one's home in a natural disaster, receiving a diagnosis of a fatal disease—all these are examples of situations when it can take months or even years for us to reach a place of acceptance by making peace with what has happened.

Practice acceptance in small ways when you experience life's inevitable disappointments; each day provides us with countless opportunities to accept that which is beyond our control. This will help you to move more quickly to a place of inner balance and calm, should you be confronted with a major crisis. Once you have ceased resisting what life brings you each moment, you will be in a much better position to decide what action, if any, needs to be taken, and then to follow through on your decision.

ALL THE ANSWERS ARE INSIDE YOU

So many of us believe that the answers to our most perplexing problems lie outside ourselves. We look to friends, family members, teachers, psychic readers, therapists, and even radio talk show hosts to tell us what to do. We allow other people—even those we have never met—to be the ultimate authorities regarding our lives. Yet, in my years of work as a psychotherapist, I have never worked with anyone who did not already have all his or her answers within. In fact, I have been awed to discover that everyone—no matter what age, no matter how seemingly lost or confused—ultimately knows the steps to follow to return to the path of integrity, wholeness, and personal fulfillment. While many need help finding the courage to follow that path, deep down, they know exactly in which direction they must go.

The map and accompanying guidebook that reveal the path to your highest good exist in only one place—inside you. By cultivating awareness, you can learn to access and trust those internal resources as your best source of information when you come upon life's crossroads. While it is fine to gain wisdom, support, and encouragement from others, it is important to recognize that the signposts that mark your journey are located on the inner plane.

Your deeper Self can only offer assistance when you request it. Ask, and it is always given. You have the world's most gifted counselor, teacher, and mentor right inside you. Make it a habit to ask every day for whatever assistance and support you desire. Your answers are always available, sometimes in the form of an inner knowing, other times in the form of the right book or a teacher who comes into your life at the perfect time and place.

You can also look within to access the strength, wisdom, vision, courage, inspiration, creative solutions, and compassion that is always available there. For example, Ardith was a depressed woman who worked in a profession she had grown to hate over twenty years. Although she was lonely, bored, and desperately unhappy, she was terrified to make a change. Ardith was attractive, intelligent, creative, hardworking, and multitalented. Yet, whenever she began to dream of returning to school and changing professions, she was paralyzed by fear. Eventually, her life became increasingly intolerable. It was then that Ardith connected with her deeper dimension Self, and found the courage and inspiration to transform her life. Using mental rehearsal and mindfulness practices, Ardith created a new internal network that enabled her to overcome old mental blocks and make life-affirming choices. She reports that her new job and educational pursuits have brought tremendous joy into her life.

Like Ardith, you can use the support of your innermost Self to identify the path of your highest good and to find the courage to embark upon it. Using the exercises in this book, you can develop and strengthen integrated neural circuits that help you recognize and act upon opportunities to step out of your comfort zone and into exhilarating, new territory.

8

Preparing to Rewrite
a Traumatic Scene

One of the most powerful and effective ways to awaken from your spellbound state is to *briefly* revisit the moments *before* a traumatic event and neutralize its impact. This chapter provides an overview for how to identify the scenes that are holding you hostage and prepares you to rewrite them using guided imagery so they can no longer negatively affect you. A rewritten scene is not meant to replace the original memory, but rather to heal its harmful effects by building additional integrative neural pathways to understand and process the event more fully. By doing this, we reset our default mode to one that is in greater alignment with our goals and desires.

How can you locate the traumatic scenes that are still holding you hostage? It is easy to discover where you are imprisoned by your past if you begin to pay close attention to your feelings and your thoughts. Life has a wonderful way of letting us know where we are most in need of healing, by putting people and events in our path that are likely to trigger our most unhealthy reactions: these relationships and situations spotlight the parts of us that are in need of our attention. They are an invitation for personal growth, gifts in the form of contentious coworkers or difficult family members who help us identify when we are under the spell of the past. The people and circumstances causing us the greatest distress can be of great value, if we observe carefully what they evoke within us. Our emotional reactions, physical sensations, and negative thoughts reveal exactly where we are held captive by our history, and point to where and how we can cut the ties that bind us to the past.

Pay particular attention to intense, overwhelming, emotional reactions to current life situations that are distressing but not devastating. While our rational mind may say, "Certainly this situation is upsetting, but it is not the end of the world," we still can't stop ourselves from feeling as if it really *were* the end of the world. An event that should be a minor source of frustration ignites our rage; or, we respond to a somewhat stressful circumstance with terror or panic.

These seemingly out-of-control emotional reactions are accompanied by physical sensations, which we often do not recognize until we tune into our bodies and ask ourselves what we are sensing at the time. How does our abdomen feel? What sensations do we feel in our chests, in our heads, necks and shoulders, or in our legs and arms? Typically, each pattern of emotional reactivity is paired for a particular individual with certain distinguishable physical sensations. This means we can learn to identify how it feels in our bodies when we are in the grips of anxiety, anger, fear, jealousy, or whatever emotion has managed to take us over. These physical sensations can be used to identify which aspect of our past is ruling us in the present.

Patterns of emotional overreactivity are often apparent in our relationships with our partners. Unconsciously, we often select partners who behave in ways that reactivate our spells. This means that our most intimate relationships can be our most challenging, but they also provide the greatest opportunity for personal growth. Our life partners are likely to be helping us become aware of any unfinished business from the past that is impacting us in the present. For example, Ted is preoccupied with his work, and frequently spends long hours at the office. Susan is hurt and angry and feels unloved because Ted works so much. When she begs him to spend more time with her, Ted feels that Susan is being bossy and overcontrolling, and he concludes that nothing he does will ever be good enough for her. His response is to physically and emotionally withdraw from Susan. This makes Susan feel even more unloved, and she tries even harder to get him to open up to her.

What does this relationship pattern have to do with Susan and Ted's past? For Susan, Ted's long work hours trigger reminders of her father's absence from her life. Susan's parents divorced when she was little, and she always felt that her father's infrequent appearances in her life meant he didn't love her. Hence, she overreacts to Ted's excessive working, and is consumed by feelings of being neglected and unloved. Her outbursts mirror the way her mother treated her father. For Ted, Susan's reactions are reminders of his smothering and overcontrolling mother. Ted's withdrawal from Susan is the same defense he used to deal with his mother's intrusiveness. Susan's eruptions are also reminiscent of his father's disapproval of him—hence the irrational conclusion that nothing he does will ever be good enough for Susan.

Ted and Susan are stuck because their spells—their negative trances—color their perceptions and expectations of each other's behavior and control their reactions. This keeps them repeating a familiar but unsatisfying relationship cycle. As Ted and Susan deal with their own unhealed traumas, they will be free to see each other's behavior through clear lenses, to hold more positive expectations, and to respond to one another in new and more creative ways.

It is not just in our home lives that we become emotionally triggered by situations that match the template of our unresolved traumas. In my consulting work with corporations, I have seen many examples of how painful experiences from the past can color and distort an employee's relationships with colleagues. For example, Don is extremely jealous of the attention given to his coworker Mark, who has been recognized for being an outstanding performer on the company's sales team. The more attention Mark receives for his accomplishments, the more inadequate Don feels. He avoids all contact with Mark and privately tries to sabotage Mark's success whenever possible. Don's reaction to Mark is due, in part, to the old wounds he carries in relation to his family of origin. Don's brother, Kevin, was the star quarterback on the high school football team. Don was uncoordinated and overweight, and intensely jealous of his brother. He deeply resented the attention his brother received at home and at school. Don felt that his parents, teachers, and peers valued his brother more than they valued him. Whether or not this is true is irrelevant. What does matter is that these are the feelings Don carries within him. One way for Don to stop reacting negatively to Mark's successes is for him to deal with the old feelings he holds regarding his perceived lack of self-worth. Until he does this, he will continue to find himself in situations where his jealousy and inadequacy buttons are being pushed.

The first two exercises in this chapter are meant to help you recognize the unhealed traumas from the past that are affecting your life in the present. This means they are designed to help you recall your *subjective* memories for the purpose of healing yourself. At times, your *subjective* memory may be different from *objective* reality. It is important to avoid confusing one with the other. For example, you may remember being run over by a white truck, but the police detective determined that it was a blue van that actually hit you. Fortunately, to release the past and move on with your life, it is not necessary to establish what really happened during the traumatic event. Often it is not possible to find corroborating data to let you know if what you remember really occurred or not. While these exercises are not designed to help you establish what actually happened to you, they can help you locate those subjective memories or memory fragments that are holding you captive in the present. In the next chapter, you will learn how to rewrite those memories in a way that liberates you from their negative impact in the present.

For several reasons, it is often best to work with a trained psychotherapist when identifying and rewriting traumatic events. First, having someone witness your process makes the experience more valid and, consequently, heightens its effectiveness. Second, it can be frightening to revisit these traumatic events, and it is often comforting to have a safe person accompany you to those dark places within. Third, a therapist can guide you through the process so that you can focus more completely on what you are experiencing in the moment. And fourth, the therapist can ensure that you awaken from your spellbound state without being retraumatized.

What follows is an example of how one woman's extreme emotional reaction and its physical concomitants were used to detect a remnant of her past, a familiar neural pathway that had been haunting her for fifty-five years, and how this discovery enabled her to set herself free.

Carol, a dynamic, sixty-three-year-old grandmother, was surprised at her reaction to the divorce of her daughter and son-in-law. She found herself weeping uncontrollably at the thought that her seven-year-old granddaughter, Brittany, "wouldn't have her father anymore." Carol was so upset about Brittany "losing her father" that she was unable to sleep at night or enjoy her usually active life. During the therapy session, as Carol spoke about her concerns, it struck me as odd that she should be so emotionally distraught over Brittany's loss of her father. After all, Brittany's father was going to be living around the corner from his ex-wife, and Brittany would be living with him half of the time. I also found it interesting that Carol was not nearly as upset about her four-year-old grandson's loss of his father, although she was very close to the boy. These clues led me to suspect that Carol was under the spell of her unresolved past.

I asked Carol to close her eyes, relax, and focus on the feelings she was having *in her body* about Brittany losing her father. Carol identified a nauseous feeling in her stomach, a tightening in her throat, a sharp feeling in her chest, and a swirling sensation in her head. Then, I asked Carol to go back to a time in her childhood or adolescence when she felt the same feelings in her body. Carol began to sob uncontrollably as she recalled having the same feelings in her body as a seven-year-old when she learned that her father had been killed in an auto accident. She continued to cry deeply over the death of her father. Through her tears, she explained that, at the time of his death, everyone told her to be strong for her mother. Being strong meant shedding no tears. There in my office, fifty-six years after his death, Carol cried *for the first time in her life* over the death of her father. And it was her granddaughter's "loss of her father" that reminded her of her own loss at the same age.

In addition to encouraging her to grieve, I guided Carol in finding and nurturing the seven-year-old child inside of her. That child had been waiting to hear that she didn't have to be strong for anyone, that it was okay for her to express her sadness.

The next time I saw Carol, she reported that she was feeling significantly better. Although she was sad that Brittany's parents were divorcing, she no longer felt overwhelmed with grief over the event. She was sleeping soundly at night and enjoying life again. Carol had healed wounds she had been carrying for over half a century by revisiting a scene in her childhood that had been left unresolved for her. By deactivating the emotional charge associated with the death of her father and creating an alternate circuit, she was able to feel and respond differently in the present.

In exercise twelve, you can use your present emotional triggers and physical responses to locate any unresolved traumas that require your attention. This exercise and the next one may put you in touch with strong, painful feelings associated with early life events. If you choose to try these two exercises on your own and find that you have a strong emotional reaction, I recommend that you contact a psychotherapist to help you cope and resolve whatever issues are unfinished for you.

EXERCISE 12 USING EMOTIONAL TRIGGERS
TO LOCATE UNRESOLVED TRAUMAS

1. Close your eyes, take a few deep breaths, and imagine yourself once again in your heart sanctuary. Reassure yourself that you can immediately return to the comfort and safety of your heart sanctuary if you are feeling too overwhelmed at any time during this exercise.

2. Once you are feeling calm and comfortable, think of a situation in your present life that triggers an emotional or physical reaction within you—perhaps stronger than you would reasonably expect under the circumstances. A good example would be a situation where, even if you've told yourself that you shouldn't be so upset, you are unable to get your emotions under control. Recalling the situation may make you feel angry, depressed, scared, embarrassed, ashamed, anxious, resentful, jealous, hurt, or any other strong emotion.

3. As you focus on the emotions and physical sensations you are experiencing as you recall the situation you have identified, notice in greater detail what you are feeling in your body. Where are you feeling the emotions in your body, and how do they feel? What are the physical sensations you are having in your body and what do they feel like? Describe how your body feels in as much detail as possible. For example, notice if any parts of your body feel hot, cold, light, heavy, tight, loose, burning, tingling, aching, nauseous, swirling, or empty. If you notice how your stomach feels, ask yourself how your chest, back, legs, head, and neck feel. Scan as much of your body as you can.

4. Now go back to another time during the last ten years when you felt the same feelings. Stay with the feelings in your body and let your mind show you another time when you felt the same way. Don't try to conjure up an image—just allow it to appear. When a scene comes to mind, notice where you are, what is happening, and how you are feeling in the scene. See if you can estimate your age at the time.

5. Now go through the same process again, going back another ten years. Repeat the process until you have gone all the way back to before the age of ten.

6. Return to your heart sanctuary to reconnect with the peace and comfort there, allowing yourself to linger for as long as you like before opening your eyes and coming back to the present.

7. Chances are good that many or all the scenes you recalled during this exercise represent unresolved traumas for you. Record your experiences from this imagery exercise in your journal for use in exercises presented later in this chapter and in the next chapter.

✦

Just as you have traced your emotions and physical sensations to locate a situation from the past that still holds an emotional charge for you, the following exercise will show you how to trace a maladaptive mental model (such as you may have identified in chapter 4) to discover its origins.

EXERCISE 13 TRACING THE ORIGIN
OF A MALADAPTIVE SCHEMA

1. Choose one maladaptive schema that you would like to remove and replace with a more positive schema.

2. Close your eyes, breathe deeply, relax, and imagine you are back in your heart sanctuary. Feel the safety and the comfort of being there. Tell yourself that you can return to your heart sanctuary any time during this exercise if you are feeling anxious or distressed.

3. Now, ask your mind to take you back to the first time you began to accept this schema as reality. For example, ask your mind to go back to when you first began to feel that you didn't deserve to have what you want. When the scene appears to you, notice everything you can about it. Where are you, how old are you, what are you feeling, and what is happening?

4. Moving on, ask your Self to locate other scenes in which the maladaptive schema was reinforced or strengthened. Take note of each additional scene, asking yourself again where you are, how old you are, what you are feeling, and what is happening.

5. Return to your heart sanctuary for as long as you like to reconnect with the peace and comfort there before opening your eyes and coming back to the present.

6. Remember to write down what you have experienced during this exercise and to save these notes for later use in this chapter and the next.

EXERCISE 14 RANKING YOUR TRAUMATIC SCENES

Now that you have a list of life events that are associated with your maladaptive schema and your strong emotional reactivity in current life situations, rank those scenes so that you can prepare to revisit and revise them.

1. Return to the notes you made during exercises 12 and 13. You should have two lists of past scenes, one from each exercise. The list from exercise 12 includes events that are related to strong emotional reactions in your present life. The items on the list from exercise 13 are situations in which you formed the maladaptive schemas that impact you today.

2. Imagine a scale from zero to ten, with zero being no emotional charge, or neutral, and ten being a very strong emotional charge. Rate each item from the two lists on the scale from zero to ten. The scenes that have a zero rating should not be at all disturbing to you, while the scenes with a score of ten are highly disturbing.

0		10
neutral		maximum
no disturbance		disturbance

3. Rank the scenes on each list in order from least to most disturbing. You may note that some scenes may be grouped together because they are similar traumas that occurred repeatedly over time. For example, if you were sexually abused many times over a period of years, you may choose just one or two representative scenes to put on your list.

NEW SCIENCE NEW BRAIN NEW YOU

4. Put a star next to any scene that appears on more than one list. These may represent traumatic events that seem to be particularly powerful in the negative influence they have upon your life.

5. Save your list to use in the next chapter when you have the opportunity to begin rewriting those traumatic scenes.

As you will see in chapter 9, when we rewrite traumatic events, we invite our current, adult selves to enter the past scene and assist our younger selves by intervening on their behalf. Since many of our most impactful traumas occurred in childhood, this generally involves having our adult selves interact with the children we once were. In order to prepare yourself for this approach, it can be helpful for you to engage in a guided imagery exercise that enables you to evoke a happy memory from your childhood. This provides your current adult self and your inner child an opportunity to "meet" in a positive setting. It is also a powerful way of continuing to install positive schemas. When we tell our inner children that we love them and that they are worthy of happiness, it can create a profound shift in our experience of our own value. Often people find this exercise to be deeply moving and one that helps them to feel more self-acceptance and self-love.

EXERCISE 15 MEETING YOUR INNER CHILD

1. Make yourself comfortable, close your eyes, and begin taking long, slow, relaxing breaths. Imagine that you are again amidst the beauty, safety, and peace of your heart sanctuary. Take a moment to reacquaint yourself with this tranquil setting in all its detail. Notice the sights, sounds, smells, tastes, and sensations present there.

2. Picture yourself surrounded in your heart sanctuary with a shimmering bubble of light. Pretend that the bubble begins to float you back in time, back to a happy scene from your childhood. Allow the bubble to transport you to a joyful time when you were still a child.

3. Once you have arrived at the pleasant childhood event, notice everything you can about your younger self and what is happening in the scene. Pay particular attention to how your younger self is feeling. If you can't remember a happy scene, simply imagine one as you wish it had been.

4. Now, imagine that your present self is stepping into the scene. Perhaps the child sees a friendly stranger approaching. When you get close enough, introduce yourself to your younger self. Tell the child, "I am you, all grown up. I've come to get to know you."

5. Spend some time interacting with the child. Learn all you can about him or her. Imagine that you play together. If you and the child feel comfortable, imagine holding the child on your lap. Tell the child you love him or her, and that he or she is precious to you. Feel your heart opening to your younger self.

6. When you are ready, you may wish to make the scene of the adult and the child very little, and put it in your heart surrounded by love. Thank the images for coming. Then, come back slowly to the present, feeling clearheaded and alert.

7. Remember to record your thoughts and feelings about this experience in your journal.

What Did You Experience?

* Were there any surprises for you?
* What did it feel like to connect with that child within?

- How might you continue to foster that connection?
- What might you do to open your heart even more to your child self?

9

Rewriting a
Traumatic Scene

Your imagination is one of your most powerful tools for awakening from your spellbound state. When you revisit a distressful episode in your imagination, you have the opportunity to set things right. You can create the scene just the way you would have liked for it to have been. You can finish the unfinished, and resolve the unresolved. You can say the things you would have liked to have said, and do the things you would have liked to have done. In rewriting a painful event, you transform it so that it no longer has power over you. The only requirement is a willingness to engage your imagination.

In my years of practice as a psychotherapist, I have found the guided imagery process described in this chapter to be one of the most powerful, healing, transformational experiences that I have ever used with clients. Time after time, people indicate that after going through this process, it has had a major, transformative effect on them. In most cases, they find themselves no longer reacting in situations that had originally triggered strong emotions. Many of them begin to chart a new life course following the process of rewriting an important traumatic event—suddenly able to do what they could not do before. They find themselves attracting new jobs, new relationships, and other new opportunities into their lives. They report feeling lighter, liberated, clear, and able to find more joy in their present lives.

The PRISM Model

The PRISM model provides a template for rewriting a traumatic scene to awaken from a spellbound state. This model enables the brain to rewire, generating new, integrated pathways that permit bright rays of sunlight to permeate the clouds of emotion that have previously distorted our vision. The PRISM model offers a means to restore our personal power, replace our maladaptive schemas, renew our sense of wholeness, and replace old coping strategies with new ways of responding that emerge from a newly integrated brain.

During the initial trauma, a person will	experience strong emotions
	feel like a powerless victim
	form maladaptive mental models
	lose parts of the self
	employ coping strategies

Using the PRISM model, a person can	*process* negative emotions
	reclaim personal power
	install new mental models
	synthesize divergent parts
	modify our default settings

When we rewrite a traumatic scene using the PRISM approach, we use our imagination to go back *to moments before the traumatic event took place. It is not necessary to relive the traumatic event itself.* We become familiar with what is happening and how our younger selves are feeling. Then, we bring our current adult selves into the scene, and we make certain that they are the most powerful people in the scene. We encourage our present adult selves to right the wrongs and to do whatever they need to do to create the desired outcome. During this process, we have the opportunity to express whatever feelings we have about the event and any perpetrators, to reclaim parts of ourselves that we have misplaced, to install new, life-affirming mental schemas, and to reset our default-functioning mode.

When we use this process, we are basically using a healing trance to break the spellbound trance that has held us captive. Our rewritten scene does not erase what happened, but it does allow our brains to process and integrate the painful memory in a new way that enables us to heal and move on. Our implicit memory becomes an explicit one which activates not only our limbic system but also our hippocampus and prefrontal cortex—those parts of the brain that serve an integrative function. This enables us to make new meaning of the event, to view it through alternate lenses that are the result of the newly activated neural circuits, and to ultimately complete processing and make peace with what has happened to us.

Often, people are surprised at what they discover when they revisit their traumas and view them through adult lenses. For example, one forty-five-year-old woman was haunted by the memory of a rape that occurred almost twenty-five years before. She remained afraid to leave the house, for fear of encountering the rapist. When she used her imagination to envision her present adult self at the scene of the rape, she was surprised to discover that her attacker was "just a boy." From the perspective of her forty-five-year-old self, he no longer seemed threatening to her.

Let us take a closer look at each component of the PRISM model.

PROCESSING NEGATIVE EMOTIONS

As long as a traumatic event generates an emotional charge, we remain under its spell. By neutralizing the emotions associated with a past scene, we can awaken from the trance that holds us captive. Thus, in rewriting traumatic episodes, it is essential that we involve both our minds and our emotions. Going through the process from the neck up alone is not going to have the same impact as allowing ourselves to feel all the feelings associated with the targeted event.

It is often frightening to even consider revisiting the emotions associated with a painful memory. Typically, we have spent years successfully avoiding contact with those feelings. We may fear that, once we open the door to the pain we hold within, we will drown in it. We may believe that we will fall apart emotionally if we allow ourselves to access the overpowering rage, grief, shame, or hurt that is associated with the trauma.

It is by both *feeling*, and then *releasing* the emotions we have stockpiled that we free ourselves from spellbound behavior. Some people are able to feel the emotions, but hold on to them for various reasons. This simply prolongs and intensifies the spell that the trauma has cast on them. Others believe they have released their emotions but have only avoided them by pushing them deeper into the shadows of their consciousness. Again, this only perpetuates the trance.

There is another important reason for letting go of the negative emotions we store within. These warehoused feelings affect our body chemistry, and they can literally make us sick over time. Hold on to enough bitter resentment, and you just might end up with any number of health problems. In contrast, happiness and peace of mind create the optimal state for maintaining our physical and mental health. When we release our emotional baggage, we create the space for greater serenity and increased joy in our lives.

To access the feelings associated with a trauma, it isn't necessary to relive the event. I have found that if people take themselves back in their imagination to a few minutes before the trauma actually occurred, they are usually able to feel the emotions that are connected to the scene without having to reexperience the actual episode. Let's review some of the emotions we may experience in relation to a traumatic episode.

Anger

We may hold resentment, bitterness, or rage toward someone we believe wronged us. Regardless of what that person may have done to us, we are hurting only ourselves by storing angry feelings within. What's more, until we release the anger from our past, it is likely to emerge at inappropriate times and places. And, we never know what may trigger one of our embarrassing explosions.

Grief

Often, there is tremendous grief, sadness, and pain associated with our most traumatic memories. We may store this hurt for decades, like an infected boil that festers within. As we attempt to safeguard that boil from being touched, we put more and more energy into self-protection and less and less into constructive endeavors. Although it hurts to lance the boil so that it may heal, it cannot compare with the agony and personal expense of living with the boil for years on end.

I have observed that most of us are able to feel either hurt or anger regarding our traumatic past, but have difficulty accessing both of these emotions simultaneously. Some people can cry and readily express their sadness, but they have trouble feeling any anger. Others express outrage over an event, but are unable to access the pain associated with the experience. Generally, I have found that the greatest healing takes place when we are able to feel and release the emotion that is most difficult for us to "own."

Fear

Traumatic events are generally terrifying. During these incidents, we often fear for our lives or the lives of others. We feel powerless to protect ourselves from the wrath of an angry aggressor; the explosion of a terrorist's bomb; or the deadly impact of a tornado, hurricane, earthquake, or tsunami. This terror becomes locked in our limbic system and continues to torment us until we use integrative right-brain processes to acknowledge the fear, broaden our perspective, and reclaim our sense of personal power and control.

Guilt

It is common for us to blame ourselves for the traumatic events we have endured—even when it is totally illogical to do so. We may believe that our parents divorced because we were bad, or that we deserved to be beaten by an abusive parent. We may tell ourselves, "If only I hadn't done X, then this terrible thing wouldn't have happened." Even when we made choices that ultimately hurt us, it does absolutely no good to continue feeling guilty. Certainly, we benefit from learning from our mistakes. But once we have figured out the lesson from our experience, it is essential to forgive ourselves and move on. Too often, we use guilt to needlessly punish ourselves. We must be willing to release our past feelings of guilt in order to be healthy in the present.

Shame

Often, there are feelings of humiliation, dishonor, and embarrassment associated with our traumatic past, which erode self-respect and self-worth. This toxic shame casts a dark shadow on our efforts and accomplishments. It colors everything we do as not good enough, and everything we are as devoid of value. It marks us as human garbage, undeserving of love or happiness. Shame is experienced below the neck. Many abuse survivors report that they know in their heads they are worthwhile; but in their hearts, they feel worthless. This illustrates the disconnect between the higher brain centers, such as the prefrontal cortex and the limbic system, where nonverbal implicit memories and their corresponding emotional concomitants and mental models are encoded. It also points to the need for integrating these parts of the brain so that one may experience a joining together, or alignment, of thoughts and feelings in both the head and the heart.

◆

By rewriting a traumatic scene using the PRISM model, we activate and involve both hemispheres along with the prefrontal cortex and the structures of the midbrain and lower brain regions, such that integration of the traumatic memory is attained. A sign that this has been accomplished is that the emotional charge associated with the traumatic event has been deactivated.

How do we know when we have accomplished this objective? When we are able to recall a traumatic event with emotional detachment. The charge has been neutralized when we can think about what happened without feeling the emotional tug. This does not mean we have forgotten what happened to us. It means we no longer allow that event to control us in the present.

RECLAIMING PERSONAL POWER

In rewriting traumatic episodes, we give ourselves the opportunity to feel victorious rather than victimized. We reclaim our power and use it to right any wrongs that may have been done to us or that we may have done to others. We confront our fears and take charge of our lives. Instead of experiencing helplessness, we discover what it is like to feel and be our most capable selves.

In the safety of our imaginations, and with the assistance of our current (adult) selves, we can ward off an attacker, stand up for ourselves with a bully, or rescue ourselves from a dangerous situation. We can say the words we were afraid to say, and do the things we were afraid to do. By being present and powerful in the same situation in which we once felt powerless, we break the spell and awaken to our true nature. As we access our higher brain centers, we are able to see the traumatic scene and our role in it from a new and broader perspective that promotes healing and transformation.

INSTALLING NEW MENTAL MODELS

When we rewrite our past, we also have the opportunity to rewire the early mental models we developed about the nature of our life dramas and the roles we play in them. As we revise early schemas so they reflect a more expanded view of what is possible for us in this lifetime, we free ourselves to have and enjoy what we really want.

Joni grew up in an impoverished environment with her single mother and three siblings. Often, the family lacked food and shelter. Joni recalls feeling ashamed throughout elementary school when other children made fun of her tattered, hand-me-down clothes. In adulthood, Joni found herself forever just scraping by financially, no matter how hard she worked to get ahead. By rewriting key scenes from her childhood, Joni was able to reprogram the schema that she would always have to struggle to make ends meet, and that she was undeserving of financial abundance. As Joni began to make new choices in alignment with her changing attitudes about prosperity, her financial situation improved greatly.

While rewriting past scenes, Joni also began to appreciate some of the positive ways in which her experience of childhood poverty affected her. She recognized that it made her more compassionate, more resourceful, less judgmental of others, and more willing to lend a helping hand to those in need. Her difficult childhood also made her stronger, less concerned about what other people think of her, and more courageous.

Treva, another client, was holding onto a relationship with a man who clearly did not value and respect her. In fact, he dated other women, saw her only when it was convenient for himself, and continually promised that "someday" they would be together. Treva had waited eight years for this to happen, and things were continuing to get worse, not better. Although she felt used and taken advantage of, she continued to hang on to this relationship.

As she worked through the PRISM model, Treva realized that she did not feel she deserved better because she had a disabled sister who would never have the opportunity to marry and have a family. At a deep level, Treva had come to feel that having a joyful relationship with a man was a betrayal of her sister. After rewriting the early scene when Treva had come to unconsciously accept this maladaptive schema as the truth, she quickly found the courage to end the relationship that was clearly going nowhere. To her surprise, soon thereafter a wonderful man she had known for years, asked her out, and things just clicked with the two of them. When last I saw her, she was thriving in a mutually loving and respectful partnership that was everything she had hoped for.

SYNTHESIZING DIVERGENT PARTS

Still another component of rewriting traumatic episodes is finding and reintegrating our lost parts. As discussed in chapter 4, during painful episodes, we often lose contact with positive aspects of ourselves. We may forget how to play, or find it impossible to trust another, or feel disconnected from sexual pleasure. When we revisit painful episodes, we have the opportunity to restore our sense of wholeness by accessing and claiming those qualities that have been misplaced in the shadows of our psyches. We can discover a capacity for courage, joy, love, creativity, intimacy, and aliveness that we never realized we possessed. Ultimately, this leads to a newfound sense of wholeness and aliveness.

MODIFYING OUR DEFAULT MODE SETTINGS

As scenes are rewritten, and we are empowered to deal with difficult circumstances in new and more effective ways, we are able to let go of automatic, limiting, coping strategies that are no longer needed. With our newly integrated neural pathways, we become free to express more of the fullness of our being, and discover alternate, life-affirming, and creative ways to respond to life's inevitable challenges.

Rosa Rewrites Her Past

The following case illustrates how rewriting a traumatic scene using the PRISM model can help us awaken from a spellbound state and restore our emotional vitality.

Rosa is a bright, attractive young woman who has years of experience working in a busy airport as a reservations agent. She sought my assistance following a distressing incident in which an angry, older male customer began to scream at her that she was an "incompetent idiot." The harder she tried to help the man, the louder and more unruly he became. Even his wife tried to calm him down, but to no avail. Normally, Rosa is able to deal with the most difficult customers in a calm, polite, and professional manner. But in this situation, she found herself trembling, paralyzed with fear, and unable to take appropriate action. As coworkers came to her aide, she burst into tears and ran back to the employee break room. There, she continued crying and shaking uncontrollably for many hours. The next day, she was overcome with anxiety any time she saw a man who even slightly resembled the one who had yelled at her.

In my office, I instructed Rosa to close her eyes, relax, and then identify the feelings in her body associated with the man's verbal attack. We then traced those feelings back to another time and place when she felt the same feelings in her body. Rosa immediately began to cry as she described a familiar scene from her early years in which her father was violently beating her mother, after Rosa's mother had simply offered him something to eat.

We rewrote the scene by having Rosa's present, empowered, adult self step into the scene (before the violence began) and prevent her father from hitting her mother. After letting little Rosa know she was there to help her, adult Rosa threatened to call the police and have her father taken off to jail if he laid a hand on her mother. Then she told him how his past behavior had affected her. She expressed her anger, hurt, confusion, and hatred toward him for the countless incidents of abuse she had witnessed against her mother. Finally, she banished him from the house forever.

Rosa then loved and nurtured her younger self, telling her the things she most needed to hear. Lastly, she addressed her mother, expressing her love, and saying how sorry she was to see her mother allow herself to be the victim of her father's abuse.

Next, we returned to the present, and Rosa continued to restructure her maladaptive neural pathways by reimagining (rewriting) the scene with the verbally abusive customer to reflect the way she would have liked to handle it.

When Rosa opened her eyes, she reported feeling tired but good, lighter and clearer. She explained to me that her mother had eventually found the courage to take her five children and leave her violent husband. We talked about what positive qualities Rosa developed as a result of what she experienced in her childhood: strength, closeness with her siblings, compassion, and determination to have a loving and harmonious marriage (which she does) and to be a great parent (which she is)!

The following week, Rosa returned to report that she was feeling great, had more energy than usual, and a pervasive sense that something had been lifted. What's more, the abusive man had returned to her workstation, and Rosa was able to deal with him appropriately, without having any emotional reaction triggered within her. To her surprise, she found herself feeling sorry for him and his wife. And she no longer felt anxious when she spotted a man who resembled the offensive customer.

Rosa's report is typical for those who have rewritten a key traumatic scene. Most say they feel clearer, lighter, and as if something has been lifted from them. Although people usually feel very tired at the end of the session, a few days later, they often experience a new supply of energy and vitality. They experience how good it feels to liberate themselves from the spell of the past and become fully alive again.

EXERCISE 16 USING THE PRISM MODEL
TO REWRITE A TRAUMATIC MEMORY

You will need to allow at least thirty minutes for this process. Choose a time when you are certain not to be interrupted. Also, make sure you are in a place where you can speak, yell, or cry in private.

As stated earlier, I recommend that you work with a therapist when doing this process. If you choose to work alone, you may want to record the instructions for yourself, leaving plenty of long pauses so you can follow along without having to open your eyes and read what to do next.

Now, review the ranked lists you created in exercise 14. From either of the two lists, choose a scene that you rated between three and five on the emotional disturbance scale. You are now going to have the opportunity to rewrite that memory.

1. Make yourself comfortable, close your eyes, take some slow, deep breaths, and imagine you are again in the safety and comfort of your heart sanctuary. Picture it in detail, using all your senses. Feel its peace and protection envelop you at every level of your being.

2. Going back in your imagination to just minutes before the scene you have identified, find your younger self and notice everything you can about where he or she is, who else (if anyone) is present, what is happening, and how your younger self is feeling.

3. Next, imagine that your present, adult self steps into the scene. Tell your younger self who you are and that you have come to help.

4. Using your imagination, make certain that your adult self is the most powerful force in the scene. You may choose to make yourself ten feet tall and carrying a magical weapon, or

picture yourself with divine protection. However you do it is okay, as long as you can feel and be the most powerful person in the scene.

5. As you stand in your power, intervene to protect your younger self in whatever way you wish. Take this opportunity to tell anyone else present how you feel about what is happening or is about to happen. (Either your younger or older self can do this.) It is best if you actually speak out loud rather than just in your imagination. Know that it is safe for you to express anything you are feeling. The more you are able to access and verbalize all your emotions, the better. Feel yourself releasing your feelings, once and for all.

6. Next, tell your younger self (out loud) whatever he or she needs to hear to be healed from this event. For example, you may want to say "This was not your fault," or "You didn't deserve to have this happen to you." Promise to always love and protect him or her from now on.

7. You may recognize some maladaptive schemas that are related to this event. Here is an opportunity to change them. For example, you can change "I am worthless" to "I am worthwhile" by talking (out loud) to your younger self and explaining why it is okay to believe or feel something different now. Imagine a whiteboard, with the old schema written on it. Erase it together and, using beautiful colors, write down the new schema.

8. Pretend you are reclaiming anything that was lost or stolen from your younger self during the targeted scene. This will probably be an abstract quality, like trust in one's self or others, joy, or spontaneity. Imagine an object or symbol that represents the quality you are reclaiming. You may wish to announce to those present in the scene what you are reclaiming and why you are reclaiming it.

9. You can also give back anything to the offender(s) that you do not want. It may be something you have been carrying for all the years since the traumatic event. For example, you may wish to give back the pain or fear they caused you, or your doubt in your own self-worth. Allow an image of a container to appear. Whatever form it takes is perfect. Then, put anything the offender gave you that you do not want in that container, seal it, and return it to the offender.

10. If appropriate, you can rewrite the entire scene from start to finish, righting any wrongs that have been done by you or to you by others. You can create a new memory in which everything happens just the way you would have liked for it to happen.

11. Take action to ensure that your younger self is safe and contented. It may feel good to leave your younger self in the new scene you have created. Or, you can imagine you are taking your younger self home with you, or to your heart sanctuary. Do whatever feels best.

12. Identify any ways in which this event helped to make you a better person. What are the positive qualities you developed as a result of this life experience? Allow yourself to experience gratitude for these.

13. Consider what you are now free to do, that you weren't free to do before. Picture yourself expressing the highest and best within you in all you do.

14. Slowly and gradually, come back to the present. Allow yourself some time for this process. Be sure to thank your imagination for assisting you with this healing process. Gradually, begin to feel your body again. Wiggle your fingers and your toes. Become aware of the sounds around you. When you are ready, open your eyes and feel yourself returning fully and completely.

15. Be sure to take time to write about what you experienced in your journal.

What Did You Experience?
- Were there any surprises?
- What was the experience like for you?
- How did you feel during the guided imagery process?
- How do you feel now?
- You may also choose to create a collage or drawing that represents your guided imagery experience in rewriting the traumatic scene.

The goal is to use the process outlined above to rewrite several of the traumatic scenes you ranked in exercise 14. Begin by rewriting the scenes that have a lower ranking on the scale of disturbance, and gradually introduce the higher ranked scenes. Scenes you starred are particularly important to rewrite.

◆

You may find that after rewriting one representative scene, the emotional charge is gone from other similar memories as well. For example, if you remember the many times you were called "stupid" by members of your family, it may be necessary to rewrite only one particularly memorable incident in order to receive optimal benefits. As you work on that one event, others, which are similar, may also lose their negative hold on you.

If you were able to become fully emotionally engaged in the guided imagery when rewriting a particular traumatic memory, it is usually not necessary to repeat the process. However, if you had difficulty becoming emotionally engaged, it may be necessary to repeat the guided visualization for that particular scene one or more times for optimal results.

Allow some time between guided imagery sessions in which you rewrite traumatic memories—anywhere from a week to more than a month. In this way, you give yourself the opportunity to fully process and integrate the experience, prior to working on another event that still holds an emotional charge for you.

Healing Is Always Possible

Ruth is a lovely woman in her sixties who worked with me in therapy to heal the emotional wounds from abuse she suffered in childhood. When it came time for us to terminate our work together, she had a dream in which she entered a small building known to house a child who had experienced "terrible injuries that broke her into pieces." In the dream, her fear was that there would be nothing left of the child. To Ruth's amazement, as she stepped into a darkened room, she saw a pedestal with a bell jar on top of it, filled with a beautiful liquidlike substance that she knew to be the child's soul. Upon seeing the spirit of the child, she fell to her knees and whispered, "I see you," gazing in reverence and awe at the most beautiful, perfect, pure, clear, radiant light she had ever seen. As the child's spirit glowed in a multitude of colors that illuminated the room, Ruth knew that she was in the presence of something very sacred.

Ruth's dream reassured her that none of the abuse she had endured had harmed the beauty and perfection of her essence. Like Ruth, you have the capacity to heal yourself and your life, for nothing you have endured in life has marred the essence of who you are, or dimmed the light that shines forever brightly at the center of your being.

Cultivating Loving Relationships

I t is generally in our closest relationships with others that we are most challenged to avoid falling into spellbound patterns. In this chapter, you will learn what you can do to alter the troublesome dynamics that continue to reappear in your relationships with certain individuals.

Our intimate relationships provide some of the best opportunities for fostering our personal growth. Much to our dismay, they force us to come face-to-face with those qualities within ourselves which are less than favorable, such as grudge holding, self-centeredness, laziness, jealousy, insecurity, the tendency to be critical, the need to be in control, the need to be right, and the tendency to feel sorry for ourselves. While it is easy to be oblivious to these undesirable qualities within ourselves when we're single, it is much more difficult to do so when we are in an intimate partnership.

At the same time, close relationships also call upon us to exercise compassion, understanding, and forgiveness. In this way, they offer us the opportunity to be our best selves. They challenge us to let go of grievances, develop empathy, practice generosity and kindness, and open our hearts to those who may have hurt us. They also teach us to be self-respecting, to find our voice, to express our needs and wants, and to set boundaries in a manner that is assertive rather than passive or aggressive.

The biggest mistake most people make when they are having problems in a relationship is to focus on blaming and trying to change the other person. This only perpetuates the relationship difficulties. Although both parties are always contributing in some way to the areas of conflict, focusing on the other person is not helpful. However tempting it may be to see the other person as being entirely at fault for the problems you are having, this will not help transform the troublesome patterns. *Your power lies in changing yourself!* And when you change yourself, your relationship will change, too.

How do you go about changing yourself to improve your relationships? It begins with practicing *relentless self-honesty*. This means that you look at yourself in the mirror and you face squarely whatever you see there. It takes tremendous courage and humility to do this. After all, none of us want to admit to those qualities that are less than favorable. It is so much easier to focus on the deficiencies in others than those in ourselves! So often, we deny our own negative traits, or project them on to others. I can't tell you how many times I have counseled couples where one is accusing the other of being critical and, in the process, being highly critical of his or her partner. In other words, we often focus on those negative qualities in others that are actually identical to our own worst traits. So, the mate who is self-centered accuses the other of self-centeredness. The one who is judgmental accuses the other of being judgmental. The unforgiving partner accuses the other of holding grudges.

As you look in the mirror and honestly admit to what you see there, it is also important to take responsibility for your part in the relationship difficulties. When we *accept personal responsibility*, we focus our energy and attention on what we can do to heal our selves and improve our lives. Rather than pointing the finger at others, we ask what *we* are doing to contribute to the problems, and what we need to change. We address our deficiencies, and build upon our strengths. We recognize that we have choices, and hold ourselves accountable for our actions. This does not mean we are hard on ourselves and fail to forgive ourselves for our shortcomings; nor does it mean that we live in the past and berate ourselves repeatedly for our failures. It is important to be gentle with ourselves, to acknowledge our mistakes and learn from them, to forgive ourselves, and to focus on making improvements in the present. When we assume personal responsibility, we demonstrate our intention to profit from life's challenges by strengthening our character, becoming more humble, and addressing our deficiencies.

Cultivating Loving Presence

Perhaps you have heard sayings such as "Love is a verb," or "Practice giving what you most want to receive." When it comes to our most intimate relationships, these messages have great value. We cannot create the kind of relationship we desire most by focusing on what we are getting; but we *can* do so by placing our attention on what we are bringing to the table. David Richo, author of the excellent book *How to Be an Adult in Relationships*, suggests that the key to having a healthy adult relationship lies in practicing mindful presence by offering the five As: attentiveness, acceptance, appreciation, affection, and allowance.[1]

When we are attentive to our partners, we are fully present and interested in what they have to say. We care about their thoughts and feelings, and we are open to hearing them. This means we make time for our partners and give them our full attention rather than engaging in conversations with them while watching the television, checking our e-mail, or thinking about our current project at work. It also means we don't walk away when our partner begins to tell us something that is difficult for us to hear.

Holding the quality of acceptance means we realize that our partners are not perfect, and we do not expect them to be so. Rather than trying to change them, we put down the chisels we use to try to sculpt them into our idea of how they should be, and offer them the gift of the freedom to be themselves.

Appreciation is the opposite of being critical; it is focusing our attention on the strengths, positive traits, and unique qualities that our partners bring into our relationships. It is being grateful for the things they do, and for who they are. As most of us know, this is much easier to do early in our relationships, before little things—like the way they leave the toothpaste cap off the tube—begin to grate on us!

Affection is expressing love in its many forms. As author Gary Chapman writes in his book *The 5 Love Languages*, each of us has our own preferred manner of expressing and receiving affection.[2] Some of us prefer physical touch, others affirming words. Some like to give and receive thoughtful gifts, others to give and receive service—like washing the car, fixing a broken pipe, or making a nice meal. Giving and receiving quality time is one more love language according to Chapman.[3] None of these are better than the others; what is important is that we learn to recognize our own love language and that of our partners, so we can express affection in a way that is most meaningful to them.

Allowance is the absence of the effort to control, dominate, or manipulate our partners. When we allow, we give our partners the space in our relationships to develop themselves, pursue their dreams, and express their uniqueness in the world in ways that make their hearts sing.

Like the other mindfulness approaches discussed in chapter 7, when we practice loving presence, we become intentionally conscious of how we are behaving in our relationships and of what our deeper motivations are for the things we say and do. We strive to be the most loving partners we can be, while recognizing that we will sometimes fall back into old automatic patterns and maladaptive neural circuits associated with our spellbound state. Each time we monitor our thoughts, feelings, and behavior, and offer kindness and compassion to ourselves no matter what we observe, we become more awake and less likely to revert to unhealthy spellbound reactions.

For example, perhaps you are striving to be appreciative and accepting of your partner, but in practicing mindful awareness you notice that you are feeling hurt and angry, and your mind is dwelling on your partner's shortcomings, determined to make him or her behave the way you intend. Just observing these thoughts and feelings from the place of a nonjudgmental witness is an enormous step in the right direction. For each time you do so, you activate the hippocampus and prefrontal cortex, and build new pathways of integration that help you to view your circumstances through clearer and more expanded field of vision. As you witness your critical and controlling thoughts with self-compassion—for these emerge from a place of fear and hurt within—you dissipate their power and make it easier to act in alignment with your goal of loving presence.

SEE Self Inquiry Model

As with other aspects of our spellbound behavior, the more conscious and aware we become of what we do and why we do it, the more we can engage our integrative higher brain centers to modulate emotional reactions and to make healthier behavioral choices. Toward this end, David Richo suggests that whenever someone else's actions or words trigger a reaction in us, we pose three questions to ourselves using his SEE (shadow, ego, early issues) model.[4]

IS THIS MY *SHADOW*?

Each of us has a shadow side that contains all the qualities— positive and negative—that we are reluctant to "own." As long as we deny these traits—particularly the negative ones—we are likely to find ourselves acting out in ways that are unhealthy and seemingly out of our control. As has been said, "What we don't own, owns us." One way that we deny our negative shadow traits—such as envy, hatred, anger, feelings of superiority, self-centeredness, or the need to be right—is to project these traits on those closest to us. That means we are blind to these qualities in ourselves, while we "see" them in others and judge those individuals harshly for having those particular characteristics. It is important that we take a careful look within to determine if we are projecting our shadow traits on our significant others. Should that be the case, it is by accepting these negative qualities as a part of who we are that we stop them from having such a powerful hold on us. We might also be projecting the positive traits that we have disowned onto others, whom we then admire or idealize. It is equally important that we "own" such qualities as our assertiveness, resiliency, wisdom, creativity, and personal power,

137

as these represent our unrealized potential. (Debbie Ford's excellent book, *The Dark Side of the Light Chasers*, provides detailed instructions on how to own and accept one's shadow side.[5])

The following guided imagery exercise provides you with the opportunity to get to know more about your shadow side and to begin to accept, rather than reject, this aspect of your being.

EXERCISE 17   OWNING YOUR SHADOW

1. Find a comfortable position in which to relax. Breathe deeply and begin to let go of external distractions as you again imagine yourself in the safe, beautiful, and loving environs of your heart sanctuary. Allow all your senses to be engaged in this process. Observe the multitude of sights, sounds, smells, sensations, and tastes present in this moment as you experience the peace, comfort, and serenity of your heart sanctuary.

2. Notice that just being in your heart sanctuary affords you great clarity, wisdom, and courage. Experience yourself connecting with the strength and compassion of your inner self more and more with each breath. This is the part of you that knows you intimately, loves you completely, and sees the big picture of your life. This part of you recognizes how far you have come and wants only to help you.

3. Consider a recent time when another person's words or actions triggered a reaction in you. If you wish, affirm to your inner Self that you are willing to see and know the truth of this situation.

4. If you would like, ask your inner Self to show you if there are any shadow qualities that you are projecting onto the other person. Once you have posed the question, simply be silent and wait for the answer to present itself. You might hear a word; see the picture of an object, symbol, or event;

or just sense a response. It is also possible that you receive no response at all right now, and it will pop into your head sometime in the near future. Just be open to whatever happens and know the answer will come in the perfect form and at the perfect time.

5. If you do receive the message that you are projecting one or more shadow qualities onto this other person, avoid judging or criticizing yourself in any way. Celebrate your willingness to go deeper within and to see and know the truth of this situation. Accept and embrace this quality in yourself. It may be a quality you were criticized for having as a child, or one that you believe is bad. Whatever it is, know that the more you can accept it as a part of you—but not all of you—the less negative impact it will have on your relationships with others.

6. If a shadow quality does occur to you, allow yourself to view it from a new perspective. What are the positive aspects of that quality? For example, if you realize that you are envious of another, perhaps that envy has given you, or could give you, the motivation to improve yourself. If you find that you are lazy, perhaps that quality has enabled you to take more time to enjoy life and be healthier, rather than living a hurried, stress-filled existence. Give yourself time to ponder the ways in which this quality has helped you or might help you in some way.

7. When you are ready, return slowly to the room, feeling clearheaded, and record your experiences in your journal.

What Did You Experience?
- What did you learn about yourself during this exercise?
- Did anything surprise you?
- How might you make use of this information in your daily life?

✦

IS THIS MY *EGO*?

Our negative egos have a field day in our relationships, if we allow them to. This is the fearful part of us that likes to be in control, engage in self-pity, complain, be right, blame, be spiteful, feel like a victim, and hold grudges. Our egos are masterful at claiming their innocence and pointing the finger at our partners. Unless we are vigilant in our efforts to see and know our true motives, they deceive us about what our real "payoffs" are for our dysfunctional behavior. For example, we may stay in a relationship in which we are being mistreated, and claim to ourselves and others that we don't know why we remain and that we really want to leave. When we look more deeply within, we may discover that a part of us enjoys the drama, the sympathy we elicit from others, the opportunity to feel sorry for ourselves, or the chance to blame our partner for our unhappiness. The abusive relationship may also provide us with an excuse for not pursuing our academic and career goals.

To determine if our reaction to another's words or actions is due to one of our negative ego's needs or intentions, we may ask ourselves questions like:

* Is this about my need to control the other?
* Am I behaving spitefully, trying to retaliate, or holding a grudge?
* Am I enjoying the feeling of self-pity?
* Is it important for me to be right and judge the other as wrong?
* Did I actually provoke the other?
* Am I enjoying the other's suffering?
* Am I reacting out of jealousy of the other's success or happiness?
* Am I reacting out of a sense of superiority or entitlement?

It takes a lot of courage, humility, self-honesty, and self-awareness to answer these questions, and others like them, truthfully. None of us want to face the fact that our motives are sometimes less than honorable—that we are flawed humans, like everyone else. Yet, that is part of the truth about us, but only part of the truth. We are also honorable, loving, generous, kind, wise, and compassionate. As humans, we each have within us the very highest and best qualities imaginable, along with those that cause us shame and suffering. The key is to *avoid judging what we see within* and to own and accept both sides of our nature. Practice holding your negative traits in the light of self-compassion. Recognize that your negative ego is frightened and doing the best it can to protect you from suffering. Although its actions may actually be creating more suffering, its intentions are to help, not hurt. As we work to be better partners, we can acknowledge that we have a ways to go. We can recognize that we have shortcomings and do our best to overcome them, one day at a time. We will never be perfect, and that is not the goal. But we can grow, develop, and become increasingly self-actualized as time goes on by cultivating deeper awareness.

The next guided imagery exercise is an opportunity to explore the role of your negative ego in a situation in which another's words or actions triggered a reaction in you.

EXERCISE 18   GETTING TO KNOW YOUR NEGATIVE EGO

1. Find a comfortable position in which to relax. Breathe deeply and begin to let go of external distractions as you again imagine yourself in the safe, beautiful, and loving environs of your heart sanctuary. Allow all your senses to be engaged in this process. Observe the multitude of sights, sounds, smells, sensations, and tastes present in this moment as you experience the peace, comfort, and serenity of your heart sanctuary.

2. Notice that just being in your heart sanctuary affords you great clarity, wisdom, and courage. Experience yourself connecting

with the strength and compassion of your inner Self more and more with each breath. This is the part of you that knows you intimately, loves you completely, and sees the big picture of your life. This part of you recognizes how far you have come and wants only to help you.

3. Consider a recent time in which another person's words or actions triggered a reaction in you. If you wish, affirm to your inner Self that you are willing to see and know the truth of this situation.

4. If you would like, ask your inner Self to show you the role, if any, of your negative ego in this event. You might ask your inner Self if this is related in some way to a need or desire you have to be right, to be in control, to judge, to feel sorry for yourself, to feel superior, or anything else. Once you have posed these questions, simply be silent and wait for the answer to present itself. You might hear a word; see the picture of an object, symbol, or event; or just sense a response. It is also possible that you receive no response at all right now and it will pop into your head sometime in the near future. Just be open to whatever happens and know the answer will come in the perfect form and at the perfect time.

5. If you do receive a message about the role of your negative ego, try to avoid judging or criticizing yourself in any way. Celebrate your willingness to go deeper within and to see and know the truth of this situation. See if you can feel compassion for this part of you that is acting out of fear, shame, or insecurity. Whatever it is, know that the more you can accept it as a part of you—but not all of you—the less negative impact it will have on your relationships with others.

6. When you are ready, return to the room, feeling clearheaded and alert, and record your experiences in your journal.

What Did You Experience?
- What did you learn about yourself during this exercise?
- Were there any surprises?
- How can you make use of this information in your daily life?

✦

IS THIS RELATED TO *EARLY ISSUES* IN LIFE?

Each of us leaves childhood with a collection of hurts and unmet needs. Unconsciously, as adults, we sometimes choose partners and friends who have aspects of the parent or other caregiver who was the least able to offer us love, acceptance, or approval. (These individuals may also have many of the positive aspects of our parents or caregivers.) While spellbound, we recreate the same situations we experienced in childhood in our attempt to master these situations and to receive what we never got from our parents. This maladaptive default-functioning mode is doomed to fail and results in our continued suffering.

One way we recreate our childhood dramas is by provoking or activating those negative aspects of the significant other that resemble the behavior of a parent or caregiver. For example, your mother was overly protective and so is your spouse. Unconsciously, you behave in ways that demonstrate you are incapable of caring for yourself and that will cause your spouse to be even more protective of you. We also project qualities on to our partners that are similar to those of our parents or caregivers. If your father was disapproving and overly critical, you may view your spouse as being overly disapproving and critical, although this is not actually the case.

Typically, while under the spell of our past, our default mode is to respond to our partner as we responded in childhood to our parents or caregivers. If we ignored our parents' or caregivers' requests or demands, we do the same with our partners. If we were fearful, passive, and accommodating when our parents or caregivers demanded that we behave a certain way, that is how we are likely to respond to our partners.

143

While spellbound, we may also look to our partners and friends to provide those things that we did not receive from our parents or caregivers. We expect our partners and friends to fill the deep holes within us by providing the unconditional love, acceptance, or approval we were lacking in childhood. We may control, manipulate, or attempt to change others in order to receive from them what our parents or caregivers could not or would not ever give us. We do not recognize that this is an impossible expectation to place on others—a plan that is doomed to fail.

Fortunately, there is a way to stop repeating this unsatisfying spellbound drama in our closest relationships and reset our default mode. By using guided imagery to heal the wounds of childhood, we can liberate ourselves to have and enjoy the kinds of intimate connections with others that are truly satisfying and fulfilling for both parties.

EXERCISE 19   HEALING THE WOUNDS OF CHILDHOOD

1. Make yourself comfortable, close your eyes, and begin taking long, slow, relaxing breaths. Imagine that you are again amidst the beauty, safety, and peace of your heart sanctuary. Take as long as you need to reacquaint yourself with this tranquil setting in all its detail. Notice the sights, sounds, smells, tastes, and sensations present there.

2. If you would like, ask your mind to take you back to a time when you were a child and you needed someone to be there, but no one was. Just be open and allow your mind to transport you to that moment in time. Don't try to remember anything—the scene will come to you in perfect timing.

3. Once you have arrived at the childhood scene in which your younger self needed someone to be there, but no one was, introduce your adult self to your younger self. Tell your younger self that you have come to help him or her.

4. Notice everything you can about your younger self and what is happening in the scene. Pay particular attention to how your younger self is feeling. Open your heart to him or her. Extend love, empathy, and compassion to this younger you who is hurting badly. Allow your younger self to express his or her emotions to you. Let your younger self know it is okay to feel whatever he or she is feeling. Listen and be fully present with your younger self.

5. No one knows better than you what your younger self needs in this moment. Perhaps it is acceptance, approval, or understanding. Perhaps it is love and kindness. Perhaps it is a feeling of belonging and being safe. Perhaps it is protection from harm. Perhaps it is to be seen and known and acknowledged for the beautiful being he or she is. Whatever it is, extend to your younger self what he or she needs most in great abundance. Talk to him or her out loud. Tell your younger self the things he or she most needs to hear—things like "I love and accept you as you are," "I believe in you," "I will always be there for you from now on," "You deserve love and respect," and "I am so sorry that this has happened to you."

6. If appropriate, take action to assist or protect your younger self.

7. Whatever your younger self is hoping to receive from his or her caregivers is never going to be forthcoming. You know this. They give what they are capable of giving, and they do what they are capable of doing. They have limitations. Help your younger self to come to accept that what he or she needs can and will come from you. To try to get it or demand it from caregivers or current life partners is to live only in frustration and unhappiness. Promise to give your younger self what he or she is trying so hard to get from others—beginning right now. This is very important and pivotal to awakening from your spell in your closest relationships.

8. Looking through the eyes of your inner Self, who sees the big picture of your life, ask yourself how your childhood challenges helped you to be a stronger or better person. What qualities did you develop as a result of what you experienced growing up? Are you more understanding, more accepting, more sensitive to others, more independent, or more certain about what you want in your life and willing to work hard to attain it? It is important to recognize the good that comes from everything we experience. There are always hidden blessings to be found in even the most painful life events, if we look for them.

9. When you are ready, you may wish to make the scene of the adult and the child very little, and put it in your heart, surrounded by love. Then come back to the present, feeling clearheaded and alert.

10. Remember to record your thoughts and feelings about this experience in your journal.

What Did You Experience?
* What was this process like for you?
* What does your inner child seem to need most from you?
* How can you offer this to your inner child on a daily basis?
* What are the clues that you can look for to let you know that your inner child is in need of your love, acceptance, and reassurance?

◆

A great way to follow-up on the guided imagery you just did is to write a letter to your inner child. You may also want to invite your inner child to respond to you. (If you do this, it is helpful to use your nondominant hand when writing the response.)

Feel free to repeat exercise 19 often, until you sense that the child within you is beginning to feel loved, accepted, whole, and complete.

In your day-to-day life, it is helpful to pay attention to when you are feeling hurt, angry, scared, guilty, or ashamed. Recognize these as opportunities to take a few minutes to close your eyes and offer love and solace to the hurting child within you. The more you practice this, the more you will notice a positive shift in how you relate to those closest to you as you establish and strengthen new, integrative brain pathways.

11

Realizing Forgiveness

Forgiveness is the most powerful medicine you possess for healing body, mind, and spirit. It is the ultimate cure for whatever ails you. The light of forgiveness transforms everything it touches. Forgiveness opens the door to miracles in your life. Forgiveness is the last step in breaking free from your past. In fact, all the processes described in previous chapters are preparation for the final act of forgiving yourself and others. When you forgive, you liberate yourself, once and for all, from the chains of the past that have bound you. Until you forgive, you may do a great job of gaining control over yourself, but it takes forgiveness to awaken completely from the spell of the past.

What does it mean to forgive? To forgive is to let go. When you forgive, you completely release whatever negative thoughts or feelings you have been holding toward yourself or another person. You say goodbye to hate, resentment, anger, hurt, guilt, and shame. You stop ruminating about how you would like to see the other punished. You cease replaying the details of the traumatic episode and telling yourself "If only . . ." Forgiveness is a powerful choice you make in order to be whole again.

Forgiving Yourself

Often, it is hardest to forgive ourselves. I have seen many clients who have easily pardoned family, friends, and strangers for any and all deliberate and unintended transgressions. They don't hold grudges against another living soul. Yet, they have refused to grant themselves the same compassion they offer so freely to others. Instead, they keep a long mental list of their own "mistakes" and use it to torment themselves. They criticize themselves from morning till night: "I should have known better," "I shouldn't have let that happen," "I should have dealt differently with that situation." They judge themselves harshly and heap upon themselves daily portions of guilt and shame. They use their mistakes as justification for the belief that they are worthless and do not deserve to be happy.

Nothing you have done is unforgivable. You are human, and by nature, humans make mistakes. We learn through our mistakes. We become better people through our mistakes. In having done things you regret, you are no different than any other person on this planet. You don't have to suffer in payment for past errors. Your mistakes can make you wiser and more compassionate. They can enable you to make better choices the next time, gain humility, and open your heart to the foibles and frailties of others.

You cannot release the past until you grant yourself the same mercy you have granted others. Until you forgive yourself, your life remains on hold. As long as you maintain stockpiles of guilt, shame, and self-blame, you are destined to remain spellbound.

One client, Michael, had been suffering from depression and an addiction to painkillers for nine years. He was barely sustaining his business, and living a lonely and sad existence in a small, dingy apartment. During therapy, I learned that Michael had never forgiven himself for an argument he had with his teenage son the night before his son died in a freak swimming accident. Even prescription drugs could not kill the pain of the guilt and self-blame Michael carried with him. His miserable life was in alignment with his belief that he deserved to be punished for his perceived wrongdoing. Nothing in Michael's world would change until he decided that he didn't need to suffer any longer. Michael was desperately in need of the most powerful painkiller of all—self-forgiveness.

SELF-ACCEPTANCE IS THE MOST IMPORTANT INGREDIENT

To forgive yourself is to release the negative judgments you have been fostering about yourself—that you are bad, stupid, shameful, disgraceful, or guilty—and replace them with self-acceptance. While negative self-judgment prevents you from moving forward, self-acceptance invites personal growth. Acknowledging your mistakes and shortcomings in an open and noncritical fashion is a major step in our personal development.

Of course, our critical minds warn us that if we accept ourselves, we won't learn from our mistakes. This is the deception. Continuing to suffer because of something we did or didn't do years ago is not learning from the past; it is using the past as an excuse for not being fully alive in the present. When we stop berating ourselves about what lies behind us, we free ourselves to create new neural pathways that lift the spell cast by our early traumas. Fairy tales abound with messages about the power of love and acceptance to awaken us from our spellbound state. Both Snow White and Sleeping Beauty are ultimately awakened from their deep sleep when kissed by a charming prince. These stories remind us not that we must find a prince to rescue us from our spellbound state, but that through the charms of self-acceptance, we can resuscitate ourselves, restore our vitality, and rediscover our zest for life.

EXERCISE 20 COMPILING A SELF-FORGIVENESS LIST

1. Make a list of all the things for which you have not yet forgiven yourself. Be honest with yourself. What do you still feel guilty, ashamed, or sorry about? What are you angry with yourself about? Do you berate yourself for something you did or did not do in the past? What do you most regret?

2. Rank your list according to how distressing each item is for you. List items from the least distressing to the most distressing.

3. For each item, write down all the things you have learned from the experience. How did it make you a better person? How are you different today as a result of the experience?

4. Next, choose something on your list that you are ready to heal and release. You can use the following exercise to forgive yourself and let go of the past.

◆

EXERCISE 21   FORGIVING YOURSELF

1. Close your eyes, take a few deep breaths, and picture yourself in the peace, comfort, and beauty of your heart sanctuary. Use your senses to fill in all the details of that sacred inner space.

2. Picture your younger self in a past scene or situation for which you would now like to forgive yourself. Recall the scene as vividly as you can in your imagination. Engage all your senses. (The scene you imagine may be representative of a series of events.)

3. Take the perspective of your younger self in that scene. Recall how it felt to be your younger self in the situation you are recreating.

4. Imagine that your present-day self steps into the scene. View your younger, less-developed self through eyes of wisdom, understanding, and compassion.

5. Tell your younger self, out loud, that you are choosing to forgive him or her for the choices he or she made. Explain how his or her mistakes enabled you to learn and grow. Express your willingness to let go of negative judgments and painful emotions you have harbored against your younger self.

6. Feel yourself becoming lighter and freer as you release all the negativity you have been carrying regarding your younger self in this situation. Feel your heart overflowing with love for your younger self. Acknowledge his or her inherent beauty and goodness.

7. If you wish, you can rewrite the entire scene, imagining everything the way you would have liked for it to have been.

8. When you are ready, return to this time and place, feeling clearheaded and alert, and knowing that you have taken an important step in your own healing.

9. Record your thoughts and feelings from this exercise in your journal.

What Did You Experience?
- Were there any surprises?
- What was the experience like for you?
- How did you feel during the guided imagery process?
- How do you feel now?

Use this process for each of the items that you listed in exercise 20. Repeat this exercise as many times as you need to for each item, until you have forgiven yourself completely.

❖

In my experience, we often forget what it was like for us at the time when we did something we have deemed unforgivable. It can help to revisit the time and place when this happened to gain a new perspective. For example, one woman had never forgiven herself for remaining in a relationship for several years with a man who was mean to her daughter. When we did the Forgiving Yourself exercise together, she suddenly recalled what it was like for her at the time—to be twenty years old with no job, no education, terrible self-esteem, and a three-year-old daughter to care for. She came to realize that although she would make a different choice today, she did the best she could at the time. This realization enabled her to finally forgive herself, after carrying the shame, guilt, and self-judgment around for decades.

If you believe you have wronged, offended, or mistreated another person, you may also choose to make amends to the individual whom you believe you have hurt. This is not a requirement for self-forgiveness, but it is an option, if you feel within that it is the right thing for you to do.

Forgiving Others

Many people hold misconceptions about forgiving others that make it difficult for them to take advantage of this potent medicine. Let's look at seven common myths about forgiveness.

MYTH NO. 1
The other person has to ask
before I can forgive him or her.
Sometimes we don't forgive someone because we are waiting for the other to ask for forgiveness, express remorse, take responsibility for bad behavior, or make restitution. This is the equivalent of putting the power to heal yourself in the hands of the person who has ostensibly wronged you. You may spend the rest of your life waiting for this other person to change, all the while suffering the consequences of remaining permanently spellbound.

Similarly, a person need not be present in order for you to forgive him or her. Forgiveness is an inside job; it is not necessary for you to communicate with the person you are choosing to forgive. Your healing need not be in any way controlled by what someone else does or doesn't do. You can choose to forgive another at any time, regardless of whether that person ever sees the light. You have the power to let go of the past and to set yourself free.

MYTH NO. 2
If I forgive, I'm saying that what the other person did was okay.

Forgiveness does not send the message that another's bad behavior was okay. For example, when we forgive someone who abused us, we aren't saying that it was fine for that person to treat us that way. Rather, we are saying that we are not going to continue to dwell on the past and carry the heavy feelings associated with the abuse. When we lighten our emotional load, the abuser cannot continue to torment us in the present.

MYTH NO. 3
I must hold positive feelings for the person I am forgiving.

Forgiving another does not necessarily mean replacing the negative feelings you have held with positive ones. When Sara forgave the stranger who brutally raped her, it did not mean that she was suddenly overcome with love for him. It did mean she was no longer going to hold on to the hatred, rage, pain, and shame that had been triggered by the attack. Forgiveness does not require placing the other in a positive light. Rather, it is the release of the negative energy you have been carrying toward the offending party.

In some cases, as we forgive, our hurt and anger melt into compassion for the other person. No one hurts another individual unless he or she is also in emotional pain. Sometimes, as we forgive, we are able to recognize the unhealed wounds of the person who harmed us. Although this doesn't make the other person's behavior acceptable, it does make it easier to forgive when we understand that the other is also under the destructive influence of ghosts from the past.

Forgiveness may help us to access love for another that has been buried under the pain. Often, the people we love the most are the ones we have the hardest time forgiving. However, forgiving is not contingent upon our being willing or able to love the person who has harmed us.

MYTH NO. 4

Forgiveness is something I do for the other.

Forgiving someone else is a gift you give yourself. It takes a lot of your energy to continue to hold on to negative feelings toward another person. Forgiveness releases this energy so you can apply it to more constructive and joyful pursuits.

Harboring bitterness, resentment, hatred, or ill will toward another is one of the most damaging things you can do to yourself. These negative emotions can poison your being, weaken your immune system, and ultimately make you sick. You needn't give someone else the power to impact your life in such profoundly destructive ways. Letting go of your negative feelings about another person is a powerful choice you can make for your own health and well-being. Forgiving someone is one of the best things you can do for you.

MYTH NO. 5

If I forgive, I will forget and be vulnerable again.

Forgiving another does not mean forgetting the things the experience has taught you. If someone mistreats you, forgiving that person does not mean you give that person the opportunity to hurt you again. It only means you are not going to carry the pain or bitterness with you any longer. You can forgive the past while holding on to its valuable lessons. Forgiving doesn't mean you are naive or unwilling to set appropriate boundaries with others. It does mean you keep the wisdom you have acquired while releasing the undesirable emotions you've accumulated along the way.

MYTH NO. 6

I only need to forgive someone once.

Forgiveness is a process that takes time. You may need to forgive someone daily for months until it feels as if you have really let go once and for all. Be gentle with yourself if you find that the negative feelings pop up again when you thought you had released them. Just affirm once more to yourself that you are choosing to let go of those feelings.

MYTH NO. 7
I need to understand why someone did what
they did before I can forgive that person.

Needing to know why someone acted badly before forgiving that individual can be a dangerous trap. Life is filled with mysteries. Often, we never know the true origins of another's behavior. To think that we need to understand before we can forgive is to remain stuck in the past for the rest of our days. You don't need to know why a person acted as he or she did in order to forgive and move on.

The Power of Forgiveness

When Tom came to see me, he was furious with his ex-wife, Lori, and had been battling with her for a year over who would keep their family home. Tom resented Lori for ending the marriage and putting him and their two sons through a painful divorce. He believed that since she had chosen to leave him for another man, he should be permitted to move back into their home while Lori found another place to live.

Tom was tired of feeling so angry and unhappy all the time. He also realized that his bitterness toward Lori was not helpful to their children. During one session, he decided that he wanted to forgive Lori, give her the house, and move on with his life. That evening, as he enjoyed his evening run on the beach, Tom had an internal dialogue with Lori, telling her that he was letting go of all bad feelings toward her and releasing the house to her as well. He was instantly overcome with a feeling of lightness and a surge of positive energy. By the time he arrived home from his run, he felt at peace within, and really good about himself and the choice he had made to forgive Lori. He noticed that the answering machine was blinking—a call had come in during his run. To his astonishment, it was Lori, saying, "Tom, I have decided that you can have the house!"

EXERCISE 22   CREATING A FORGIVENESS LIST

Make a list of all the people you believe you need to forgive. Be honest with yourself. Include anyone toward whom you feel bitter, resentful, or spiteful, or anyone you feel has hurt you deeply.

EXERCISE 23   THE RAINBOW BRIDGE

For this exercise, have one person in mind whom you are ready to forgive.

1. Close your eyes, and picture yourself in the serenity, safety, and comfort of your heart sanctuary. Breathe deeply, relaxing more and more completely with every breath.

2. Imagine that you can see a glowing rainbow, extending from your heart sanctuary up into the heavens. The colors of the rainbow are bright, clear, and radiant.

3. You notice the rainbow is a bridge you can walk on. If you choose, you can go now, slowly, to the center of the bridge, where you will meet face-to-face with the person you want to forgive. Note that you are completely safe and protected while on this bridge. No one can harm you.

4. You may notice yourself viewing this person through the wise eyes of your inner Self, or accessing the compassion your inner Self feels for this individual. Perhaps you become aware of the beauty of this person's true essence. Or, you may suddenly have a clear picture of the wounded child within this person.

5. Take time to tell this person that you are choosing to forgive him or her. Explain what feelings or judgments you have been holding on to, and why you are choosing to let them go. As you speak, the other person may only listen. If you

wish, you can ask the other to respond to you when you are finished, or engage in a dialogue. Feel yourself releasing all the emotional baggage you have been carrying around as you talk to this person.

6. As you finish speaking, a brilliant stream of pure, uplifting, healing light enters your head and torso, and dissolves any remnants of pain, anger, hatred, or resentment that you are still holding against this individual. Notice how light and free you feel.

7. Do whatever feels good to end this encounter, and return to your heart sanctuary. Come back to this time and place whenever you are ready, feeling clearheaded and alert.

8. Write about your experience in your journal. Be sure to note if there were any surprises or if you received any insights or ideas about what to do next.

What Did You Experience?
- Were there any surprises?
- What was the experience like for you?
- How did you feel during the guided imagery process?
- How do you feel now?

Repeat this process as often as necessary. See if you can meet each person you wish to forgive on the rainbow bridge at least once.

✦

Celebrating Forgiveness

We use rituals, or ceremonies, to mark life's transitions. Some common rituals in Western cultures include baptisms, marriages, funerals, and birthday parties. During rituals, we take part in activities that involve the use of symbols that have special meaning to us. For example, at a birthday party, we put candles on a cake, sing "Happy Birthday," ask the person who is turning a year older to make a wish and blow out the candles, and then cut the cake. We also bring wrapped gifts for the celebrant. Some of the activities which may be a part of a ritual include: eating, drinking, toasting, dancing, singing, exchanging gifts, bathing, wearing special clothing, playing games, reading aloud, offering blessings or good wishes, planting, burning, chanting, or praying.

We may include just one person, or hundreds, as we engage in a particular ritual. In the following case example, a woman chose to have several close friends present during the enactment of a ceremony she designed for forgiving her ex-husband and moving on with her life.

Marsha had been haunted by the bitter resentment she felt toward her ex-husband, Larry, who had left her more than ten years earlier for a younger woman. In therapy, Marsha came to realize that the hostile feelings she held for Larry were actually keeping her stuck and poisoning her present life experience. She worked hard at letting go of the hurt and anger she had been harboring for so long. And her final step in forgiving Larry and releasing all the pain she had been carrying regarding the divorce, was to design and carry out her own ritual. She wrote Larry a letter, explaining that she was choosing to let go of the bitterness she felt toward him so that she could move on with her life, thanking him for all the valuable lessons he had taught her, for the good years they had together, and wishing him well in his life. Then, she took her wedding ring, and asked a jeweler to reset the diamond into a pendant she could wear as a necklace. She invited three close female friends to her house on the anniversary of her divorce. With all present gathered in a circle, Marsha read and then burned her letter to Larry. Next, Marsha expressed her appreciation to each friend for supporting her through this process. Then, Marsha brought out her new diamond pendant and passed it around. Each friend held it, offered her blessings, and spoke of her good wishes for Marsha from this day forward. Finally, Marsha put the pendant on a gold chain around her neck and affirmed her intention to enjoy her new life and welcome new experiences. They completed the celebration by sharing a meal and a bottle of fine wine, with a toast to Marsha's health and happiness.

A ritual of your own design can be a poignant way to underline your determination to forgive yourself and others, and fully release the past. Your personal ceremony can serve as a transition point in your life, marking your passage from spellbound to free. Design your own ritual, using symbols and activities that are meaningful to you. You can invite as few or as many participants or witnesses as you wish. You can hold your rites in the privacy of your home, in a church or temple, on a mountaintop, in a forest clearing, or on the shore of an ocean or lake.

Remember, a ritual is a final step in the process of forgiveness. Imagine your surprise and delight as you feel the deep and powerful internal shift that often results from participating in your own forgiveness ceremony.

12

Expanding Your
Creative Vision

What can we expect as we clear the unresolved issues and left-over emotions from years past? How might we be different as we work through the processes from this book to awaken our ability to be fully present in the now and strengthen integrative brain pathways that enable us to think in new ways? Many report that they embrace an expanded vision of themselves and their lives—one that was not possible while they were spellbound. This new perspective opens them to a field of new possibilities. Where before they felt limited and confined, afterward there is the sense of great, untapped creative potential.

Some discover that they have gained easier access to the creative stream of universal energy that flows like a great river through each of our lives. When you join that endless flow of well-being, you open to the unlimited blessings that life has to offer. Instead of repeatedly replaying the same unsatisfying themes, you find yourself in the right place at the right time, living with greater ease, joy, and satisfaction. At times, the way circumstances and events unfold with perfect timing, in alignment with your greatest hopes and fondest dreams, may even seem magical. Your life becomes an enchanting journey rather than a painful endurance test.

Living in the flow means retiring your life of struggle. You cease swimming against the current, and instead, allow it to transport you, easily and with far less effort, to your chosen destination. While you still act to accomplish your goals, your actions are fueled by inspiration and fired by passion. You no longer waste energy trying to force yourself to do what you believe you *should* do. You discover a wellspring of motivation that propels you in whatever direction you want to go.

Letting go of struggle is not easy when we have been accustomed to our critical mind urging us to struggle more and convincing us that we have to prove our worthiness with blood, sweat, and tears. Yet, as the following example illustrates, it is only when we stop trying so hard to make things happen that things often change significantly for the better.

When I met Abby, she was in dire financial straits. On an impulse, she had quit her job two years earlier in order to build her own business. Since then, despite her best efforts to grow the business, her financial situation had progressively worsened. Although she did not spend money frivolously, she was barely holding on and in imminent danger of losing the business and living out on the streets. She was deeply ashamed of having had credit cards revoked for lack of timely payment, bank accounts closed due to too many overdrawn checks, and collections agents calling to demand payment for her many debts. Abby had always been responsible with money and wanted desperately to pay all her bills. Yet nothing she had tried had improved her situation. In spite of all her prayers and hard work, things were only getting worse.

Abby confessed that she worried constantly about her disastrous financial affairs; day and night, she agonized over her lack of money and envisioned the most dire consequences. When she wasn't feeling guilty and ashamed about the past, she was living in fear of a catastrophic future.

I knew that for her financial situation to improve, Abby needed to let go of worry, guilt, and fear, and replace them with feelings of well-being. Rather than pushing so hard to try to make things better, she needed to allow good things into her life more easily. Abby had believed that if she did not spend every minute agonizing and worrying about her financial situation, it meant that she didn't care and that she was therefore being irresponsible about money.

With therapy and the use of many of the techniques described in this book, Abby eventually released her worries and fears and surrendered to the universal flow. As she placed her trust in her deeper Self, she felt at peace for the first time in many months. Abby realized that letting go of the struggle meant being willing to follow the path that her inner guidance illuminated for her. As she recognized the urge to make a phone call or write a letter, she acted upon it. To Abby's surprise and delight, her financial situation began to improve within days of stopping her intensive effort to make it better. Paradoxically, it was only when she ceased trying so hard to create abundance that greater and greater amounts of money began to flow into her life in amazing ways. Within three months, Abby had all the new business she could manage, her income had tripled, and she was well on her way to paying off all her debts.

The following guided imagery will assist you in opening to your highest good as you release the need to struggle.

EXERCISE 24   OPENING TO RECEIVE LIFE'S BLESSINGS

1. Sit or lie down in a comfortable position, close your eyes, and begin to breathe deeply. Find yourself again in the soothing, nurturing safety and comfort of your heart sanctuary. Picture its smells, sights, sounds, tastes, and sensations. Feel the peace emanating throughout this special space.

2. Imagine that there is an expansive river of light flowing into your heart sanctuary, and it carries directly to you everything you are wanting. There is nothing for you to do but allow your highest good to come to you, easily and effortlessly, via this endless stream of positive energy. You needn't even know what your highest good looks like. Just invite it into your heart sanctuary and know that it will be perfect for you in every way.

3. Picture all that you desire filling your heart sanctuary as you open yourself to receiving abundance of every kind. Imagine that everything you have attracted brings more light into your life. Feel yourself becoming even more radiant as you harmonize your light with the many blessings that surround you.

4. Feel free to remain in your heart sanctuary for as long as you like. When you are ready, return to the present time and space, feeling clearheaded, refreshed, and alert, and record your experiences in your journal.

What Did You Experience?
* Were there any surprises?
* What was the experience like for you?
* How did you feel during the guided imagery process?
* How do you feel now?

◆

An Expanded Vision

What is your expanded vision for yourself and your life? How has awakening from your spellbound state and resetting your default-functioning mode changed the way in which you see yourself now and in the future? In what ways are you now different? How do you see yourself years from now as you continue along this pathway of healing and personal unfoldment? The following guided imagery exercise will provide you with the opportunity to begin to open to a new identity that is in greater alignment with the person you are today and the person you are becoming.

EXERCISE 25   MEETING YOUR FUTURE SELF

1. Sit or lie down in a comfortable position and begin taking slow, deep breaths. Imagine yourself in the beautiful, safe, and serene environment of your heart sanctuary. Take all the time you need to settle into yourself and relax deeply and completely.

2. When you are ready, if you would like, imagine that there is a bridge in your heart sanctuary. Waiting for you on the other side of that bridge is your future self, five years from now. This future self has met and even surpassed all your goals and dreams. He or she is glowing with radiant health, inner peace, and an overall sense of well-being. Your future self is filled with confidence and self-assurance, and is living a joyful and fulfilling life.

3. As you cross the bridge to meet your future self, what do you first notice about this person? How does it feel to be in the presence of your future self? What surprises you most about him or her? Take all the time you need to communicate with your future self. Get to know more about how it feels to be that person. Ask questions if you wish, or just absorb the love and appreciation your future self has for you. Everything you have lived has enabled your future self to be the person he or she now is. Your future self recognizes and acknowledges the courage, determination, and focus you have demonstrated in healing your past and moving beyond it.

4. Your future self has a gift for you that is based upon his or her intimate knowledge of you and your circumstances, coupled with deep compassion for you, what you are going through, and what you need most at the present time. If you would like, receive that gift now.

5. Additionally, as you prepare to cross the bridge, keep in mind that your future self is *you*, and already resides within you. That means you can always call upon him or her to access greater strength, confidence, courage, wisdom, insight, or whatever you may need in your current life circumstances.

6. When you are ready, thank your future self for meeting with you, recross the bridge and slowly return to this time and place.

7. Once you return to the room, begin to wiggle your fingers and toes and notice yourself feeling clearheaded and alert. Take time to record your thoughts and feelings regarding meeting your future self in your journal.

What Did You Experience?

- Did anything surprise you about this meeting?
- Was there a gift from your future self? If so, what meaning does this have for you?
- What are you free to do now that you weren't free to do before?
- How does this experience change your view of yourself and your life?

✦

Final Words

As you use this handbook to awaken from your spellbound state, remember that our lives follow seasons like the earth that sustains us. When you are in a winter mode, you may feel frozen and barren, and wonder if there will ever be a time of new growth. Or, you may feel peaceful and content, hibernating for a while in preparation for the coming spring. Even though it appears as if there were nothing much going on during your wintertime, seeds of change are taking root beneath the surface. A winter may last weeks, months, or years for you.

But eventually, spring always arrives, bringing glorious color and an explosion of new creativity and life. Spring is when you begin to enjoy the results of cultivating new ways of thinking, feeling, and behaving. By summertime, you are basking in the light of your personal unfolding, like a beautiful flower whose petals are drinking in the sun's life-giving rays. With the coming of fall, enjoy the harvest that already bears the seeds for the new planting. While the old is slowly dying off, new opportunities appear for planting these seeds in the fertile soil of your consciousness. And then, of course, another winter arrives.

Find pleasure in each season of your journey toward greater aliveness and wholeness. Be gentle with yourself. Learn to move according to your own rhythm, doing what feels right and good to you at your own pace. Take your time to savor the delight and perfection of wherever you are in nature's gentle unfolding as you experience the ebb and flow of consciousness that accompanies life's seasonal changes.

May this book accompany you through the darkest winter and the brightest summer. Let it guide you back to your Self, should you temporarily find yourself lost in a storm of emotion. Use it to rake away the dead leaves of fall and to recognize the first tiny buds on a young tree in early spring. Let it remind you to celebrate yourself and your profound connection to all life. Most of all, may it help you to awaken to who you really are—Love itself.

Notes

CHAPTER 1

1. Rick Hanson and Richard Mendius, *Buddha's Brain: The Practical Neuroscience of Happiness, Love, and Wisdom* (CA: New Harbinger Publications, Inc., 2009); Daniel Siegel and Mary Hartzell, *Parenting from the Inside Out: How a Deeper Self-Understanding Can Help You Raise Children Who Thrive* (New York: Jeremy P. Tarcher, 2004).

2. Bessel A. van der Kolk, "Trauma and Memory," in *Traumatic Stress: The Effects of Overwhelming Experience on Mind, Body, and Society*, eds. Bessel A. van der Kolk, Alexander C. McFarlane, and Lars Weisaeth (New York: Guilford Publications, 2007); Daniel L. Schacter, "Implicit Memory: History and Current Status," *Journal of Experimental Psychology: Learning, Memory, and Cognition* 13, (1987): 510–518.

3. Siegel and Hartzell, *Parenting from the Inside Out.*

4. Schacter, "Implicit Memory: History and Current Status"; Siegel and Hartzell, *Parenting from the Inside Out.*

5. van der Kolk "Trauma and Memory"; Siegel and Hartzell, *Parenting from the Inside Out.*

6. Siegel and Hartzell, *Parenting from the Inside Out.*

7. Rick Hanson, *Hardwiring Happiness: The New Brain Science of Contentment, Calm, and Confidence* (UK: Rider, 2013).

8. Donald. O. Hebb, *The Organization of Behavior: A Neuropsychological Theory* (New York: John Wiley and Sons, 1949).

9. Siegel and Hartzell, *Parenting from the Inside Out*.
10. Bogdan Draganski et al., "Neuroplasticity: Changes in Grey Matter Induced by Training," *Nature* 427 (2004): 311–312.
11. S. W. Lazar et al., "Meditation Experience Is Associated with Increased Cortical Thickness," *Neuroreport* 16 (17) (2005): 1893–1897.
12. Paul MacLean, *The Triune Brain in Evolution: Role in Paleocerebral Functions* (New York: Springer, 1990).
13. Joe Dispenza, *Evolve Your Brain: The Science of Changing your Mind*, (Deerfield Beach, FL: Health Communications, 2007).
14. van der Kolk, "Trauma and Memory."
15. Dispenza, *Evolve Your Brain*.
16. Siegel and Hartzell, *Parenting from the Inside Out*, 177.
17. Ibid.
18. John Arden, *Rewire Your Brain: Think Your Way to a Better Life* (New Jersey: John Wiley & Sons, 2010); Siegel and Hartzell, *Parenting from the Inside Out*.
19. Siegel and Hartzell, *Parenting from the Inside Out*, 179.
20. Ibid, 178.
21. Martin Rossman, *The Worry Solution: Using Breakthrough Brain Science to Turn Stress and Anxiety into Confidence and Happiness* (New York: Crown Archetype, 2010).
22. David G. Myers, *Psychology* (International Ed.) (New York: Worth Publishers, 2013).
23. Linda Graham, *Bouncing Back: Rewiring Your Brain for Maximum Resilience and Well-Being* (Novato, CA: New World Library, 2013), 41.
24. Belleruth Naparstek, *Invisible Heroes: Survivors of Trauma and How They Heal* (New York: Bantam Dell, 2004); van der Kolk, "Trauma and Memory"; Siegel and Hartzell, *Parenting from the Inside Out*.
25. Naparstek, *Invisible Heroes*.
26. Ibid.

CHAPTER 2

1. Naparstek, *Invisible Heroes*, 149–150.
2. A good resource for children's imaginary journeys is Dr. Charlotte Reznick's website www.imageryforkids.com.
3. Rossman, *The Worry Solution*.

CHAPTER 3

1. A. Pascual-Leone et al., "Modulation of Muscle Responses Evoked by Transcranial Magnetic Stimulation during the Acquisition of New Fine Motor Skills," *Journal of Neurophysiology* 74, 3 (1995): 1037–1045.
2. Ibid.
3. Ibid.

CHAPTER 4

1. Esther Hicks and Jerry Hicks, *Ask and It Is Given: Learning to Manifest Your Desires* (Carlsbad, CA: Hay House, 2004).
2. Jeffrey Young and Janet Klosko, *Reinventing Your Life: The Breakthrough Program to End Negative Behavior and Feel Great Again* (New York: Plume, 1994). Young and Klosko's book is an excellent reference for additional information about these life patterns, which they call "lifetraps."
3. Ibid.

CHAPTER 5

1. Hansen and Mendius, *Buddha's Brain*, 68.

CHAPTER 7

1. Daniel Siegel, *Pocket Guide to Interpersonal Neurobiology: An Integrative Handbook of the Mind* (New York: W.W. Norton and Company, 2010); Hanson and Mendius, *Buddha's Brain*.
2. Eckhart Tolle, *The Power of Now: A Guide to Spiritual Enlightenment* (Novato, CA: New World Library, 1999).
3. R. J. Davidson et al., "Alterations in Brain and Immune Function Produced by Mindfulness Meditation," *Psychosomatic Medicine* 65, 4 (2003): 564–570.

4. E. Luders et al., "The Underlying Anatomical Correlates of Long-Term Mediation: Larger Hippocampal and Frontal Volumes of Gray Matter," *Neuroimage* 45 (2009): 672–678.

5. Eckhart Tolle, *The Power of Now*.

CHAPTER 10

1. David Richo, *How to Be an Adult in Relationships: The Five Keys to Mindful Loving* (Boston: Shambhala, 2002), 50.

2. Gary Chapman, *The 5 Love Languages: The Secret to Love That Lasts* (Chicago: Northfield Publishing, 1992).

3. Ibid.

4. David Richo, *How to Be an Adult in Relationships*, 150–151.

5. Debbie Ford, *The Dark Side of the Light Chasers* (New York: Riverhead Books, 1998).

Bibliography

Arden, John. *Rewire Your Brain: Think Your Way to a Better Life.*
New Jersey; John Wiley & Sons, 2010.

Chapman, Gary. *The 5 Love Languages: The Secret to Love That Lasts.*
Chicago: Northfield Publishing, 1992.

Davidson, R., J. Kabat-Zinn, J. Schumacher, M. Rosenkranz, D.
Muller, S.F. Santorelli, F. Urbanowski, A. Harrington, K. Bonus,
and J.F. Sheridan. "Alterations in Brain and Immune Function
Produced by Mindfulness Meditation." *Psychosomatic Medicine*
65 (2003): 564–570.

Delunas, Eve. *Survival Games Personalities Play.* Big Sur, CA: SunInk
Publications, 1992.

Dispenza, Joe. *Evolve Your Brain: The Science of Changing your Mind.*
Deerfield Beach, Florida: Health Communications, 2007.

Draganski, B., C. Gaser, V. Busch, G. Schuierer, U. Bogdahn, and
A. May. "Changes in Grey Matter Induced by Training. *Nature*
(London) 427 (6872) (2004): 311–12.

Ford, Debbie. *The Dark Side of the Light Chasers.* New York:
Riverhead Books, 1998.

Graham, Linda. *Bouncing Back: Rewiring Your Brain for Maximum
Resilience and Well-Being.* Novato, CA: New World Library,
2013.

Hanson, Rick. *Hardwiring Happiness: The New Brain Science of
Contentment, Calm, and Confidence.* UK: Rider, 2013.

Hanson, Rick. and Richard Mendius. *Buddha's Brain: The Practical Neuroscience of Happiness, Love, and Wisdom.* CA: New Harbinger Publications, Inc., 2009.

Hebb, Donald. O. *The Organization of Behavior: A Neuropsychological Theory.* New York: Wiley, 1949.

Hicks, Esther and Jerry Hicks. *Ask and It is Given: Learning to Manifest Your Desires.* Carlsbad, CA: Hay House, 2004.

Lazar, S., C. Kerr, R. Wasserman, J. Gray, D. Greve, M. Treadway, M. McGarvey, B. Luders, E., A. W. Toga, N. Lepore, and C. Gaser. "The Underlying Anatomical Correlates of Long-Term Mediation: Larger Hippocampal and Frontal Volumes of Gray Matter," *Neuroimage* 45 (2009): 672–678.

MacLean, Paul D. *The Triume Brain in Evolution: Role in Paleocerebral Functions.* New York: Springer, 1990.

Myers, David. G. *Psychology* (International Ed.). New York: Worth Publishers, 2013.

Naparstek, Belleruth. *Invisible Heroes: Survivors of Trauma and How They Heal.* New York: Bantam Dell, 2004.

Pascual-Leone, A., N. Dang, L.G. Chen, J. P.Brasil-Neto, A.Cammarota, A., and M. Hallett. "Modulation of Muscle Responses Evoked by Transcranial Magnetic Stimulation during the Acquisition of New Fine Motor Skills," *Journal of Neurophysiology* 74 (3) (1995): 1037–1045.

Quinn, J. Dusek, H. Benson, S. Rauch, C. Moore, and B. Fischl. "Meditation Experience Is Associated with Increased Cortical Thickness," *Neuroreport* 16 (17) (2005): 1893–1897.

Richo, David. *How to Be an Adult in Relationships: The Five Keys to Mindful Loving.* Boston: Shambhala, 2002.

Rossman, Martin. *The Worry Solution: Using Breakthrough Brain Science to Turn Stress and Anxiety into Confidence and Happiness.* New York: Crown Archetype, 2010.

Schacter, D. L. "Implicit Memory: History and Current Status," *Journal of Experimental Psychology: Learning, Memory, and Cognition* 13 (1987): 510–518.

Shapiro, Francine. *Eye Movement Desensitization and Reprocessing.* New York: Guilford Press, 1995.

Siegel, Daniel. *Pocket Guide to Interpersonal Neurobiology: An Integrative Handbook of the Mind.* New York: W.W. Norton and Company, 2012.

_____. *The Mindful Therapist: A Clinician's Guide to Mindsight and Neural Integration.* New York: W.W. Norton and Company, 2010.

Siegel, Daniel and Mary Hartzell. *Parenting from the Inside Out: How a Deeper Self-Understanding Can Help You Raise Children Who Thrive.* New York: Jeremy P. Tarcher, 2004.

Tolle, Eckhart. *The Power of Now: A Guide to Spiritual Enlightenment.* Novato, CA: New World Library, 1999.

van der Kolk, Bessel A. *The Body Keeps the Score: Brain, Mind, and Body in the Healing of Trauma.* New York: Viking, 2014.

van der Kolk, B. A., A.C. McFarlane, and L. Weisaeth (eds.). *Traumatic Stress: The Effects of Overwhelming Experience on Mind, Body, and Society.* New York: Guilford Publications, 2007.

Young, J. E. and Janet Klosko. *Reinventing Your Life: The Breakthrough Program to End Negative Behavior and Feel Great Again.* New York: Plume, 1994.

Yue, G. and K. Cole. "Strength Increases from the Motor Program-Comparisons of Training with Maximal Voluntary and Imagined Muscle Contractions," *Journal of Neurophysiology* 67 (5) (1992): 1114–1123.

About the Author

Eve Delunas, PhD, LMFT, is a psychotherapist, educator, and organizational trainer with over thirty years of clinical experience in using guided imagery to help individuals recover from trauma and transform their lives. She is an internationally known speaker who has facilitated training workshops in Germany, the United Kingdom, Canada, and throughout the United States. She has taught counseling for the University of Maryland, University College, European Division, the University of San Francisco, and John F. Kennedy University. In her first book, *Survival Games Personalities Play*, Eve describes her unique approach to using the temperament model to understand and treat symptomatic behavior.

Eve and her husband, Roger, have been married for twenty-nine years. Seven years ago, they left their longtime home in Carmel/Big Sur, California, for a new adventure that has taken them throughout Europe and now Hawaii. In her free time, Eve enjoys volunteering at the Hawaii Humane Society and visiting the many beautiful Hawaiian island beaches.

To contact Eve please visit her Facebook page.

Made in the USA
San Bernardino, CA
23 September 2017